6 Essentials *to* Start & Succeed In Your Own Business

6 Essentials *to* Start & Succeed In Your Own Business

What Top Entrepreneurs Know, That Others Don't

BRIAN TRACY

MEDIA

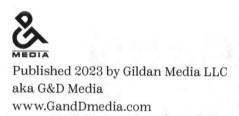

Published 2023 by Gildan Media LLC
aka G&D Media
www.GandDmedia.com

Designed by Meghan Day Healey of Story Horse, LLC.

Library of Congress Cataloging-in-Publication Data is available upon request

ISBN: 978-1-7225-0644-5

10 9 8 7 6 5 4 3 2 1

CONTENTS

CONTENTS

INTRODUCTION

Brian Tracy is one of the world's foremost authorities on business and personal success. He has given more than 5,000 talks and seminars to over five million people and is a business coach to top leaders in major industries worldwide.

In *6 Essentials to Start & Succeed In Your Own Business,* Brian will help you become knowledgeable about the best ideas for personal success, wealth, happiness, and fulfillment, and expose you to the most innovative, current, and, most importantly, proven ideas on how to become successful. *Learning and consistently applying the 6 Essentials* will be the vehicle that will take you, and your business, as Brian's late friend Zig Ziglar used to say, "all the way to the top."

You might ask why Brian chose this topic, the process of starting and succeeding in your own business, also known as *entrepreneurship*. Simply this: The world that we live in today, and the world that you will build your career in favors the person who organizes and operates a business, and takes on greater than normal financial risks to do so—the person also known as the *entrepreneur*. If you're in your twenties and thirties, you may forge a second or third career as an entrepreneur; and if you're in your forties, fifties, or beyond, you will decidedly favor the idea of starting and owning your own business.

Here are a few statistics: According to *Fortune* magazine, as of 2016, millennial entrepreneurs—what they call *millennipreneurs*, who are twenty to thirty-five years old—are starting more companies, managing bigger staffs, and targeting higher profits than their baby boomer predecessors.

Fifty-two percent of all small businesses are home-based, and many of those are started and run by people in their mid-career. Of those businesses, 75% of all US businesses are non-employer businesses, such as sole proprietorships.

According to Ed Hess, professor of business administration at the Darden School of Business at the University of Virginia, over the next ten to fifteen years, 47% of all jobs in the US are likely to be replaced by technology, more than 80 million in all.

According to the Bureau of Labor Statistics, the average worker holds ten different jobs before age forty, and this number is projected to grow. Forrester Research predicts that today's youngest workers will hold twelve to fifteen jobs in their lifetime.

What do all these statistics show? That whether you are early in your career or are in mid-career, whether you have ambitions to run a larger business or a very small business, and whether you start a business because it's your desire or you're forced to by automation and layoffs, entrepreneurship is more likely than ever to be a part of your future.

According to Brian Tracy, that's a very good thing. Just think about that last statistic, switching jobs up to fifteen times. Wouldn't it be better to own that job and have greater control over your own destiny? What's more, as Brian will explain, it has never been easier to start and run your own business.

When Brian presented *How to Start and Succeed in Your Own Business,* way back in the 1980s, the barriers to starting a business were much greater. Staffing costs, marketing costs, long-distance calling costs, the availability of startup capital, and even the infrastructure required, made running your own business a distant dream for most people. Today you can start a business with a laptop, a wireless cable connection, and a very strong LinkedIn profile.

The barriers to entry in nearly every market have been broken down. You can start a business with little or no staff. Marketing and advertising costs are being driven lower and lower. Production and distribution costs are being driven to zero. You can easily start a business from your home office, and startup capital is so accessible that websites like kickstarter.com and other crowdfunding sites have become household names. However, there is one thing that has not changed in what it takes to start and succeed in your own business—from the 1980s to today: You must learn and consistently apply the 6 Essentials that are responsible for all entrepreneurial success.

In this timely book, Brian will describe these 6 Essentials, and show you how to use this knowledge to race ahead of the competition and take advantage of all of the modern options readily available to you because of that low barrier to entry. Yes, you, starting from wherever you are today, can start your own highly profitable business, and grow that business to any size in terms of staff and revenue that you desire. Best of all, he'll teach you how to make that business successful and sustainable for the long term, so you don't become one of those unfortunate statistics in two to three years, like the vast majority of business owners.

In this brave new world, the best vehicle for reaching the top and for controlling your own destiny is entrepreneurship. Get ready, as Brian presents the "secret" formula that the majority of successful entrepreneurs follow. You can be one of them.

—Editor

1

Welcome to the Entrepreneurial Age!

Years ago, when I started off, I came from a limited background. I didn't graduate from high school. I worked at laboring jobs for years, and I struggled. I was envious of people who were doing better than me, and I began to ask why some people are more successful than others. Then I began to study economics, especially entrepreneurial economics. I found that for the last 200 or 300 years, the driving engine in our society has been the entrepreneur.

The entrepreneur is a person who sees an opportunity to serve people in some way with a product or service that they want and need, and then is able to bring this product or service to the customer at a cost that is lower than the customer is willing to pay. It's a very simple equation. I spent hundreds of hours studying this, because it's fascinating. The bottom line is that human needs are unlimited. Whatever a person has, they want something more, and they want something different.

I've written eighty-five books now, and I'm thinking of writing another. It would be called *The ER Factor*. *ER* stands for *ER*, so bett-ER, fast-ER, easi-ER, cheap-ER, and so on. You'll find that all human beings are motivated by ER. Successful companies are the ones that offer the best ER to this customer at this time in this product or service area. There are no limits to what you can do.

The fastest way for you to become financially independent and to have a wonderful life and a wonderful standard of living is to find a way to offer something that people want and need that's faster, better, cheaper, easier, and more convenient.

My favorite example is Jeff Bezos and Amazon. A couple of decades ago, even less, he drove out from New York to Seattle, and while his wife drove, he typed up a business plan, which we'll talk about later. The business plan was very simple. It's what is it that people want and need and are willing to pay for?

People love to buy books. You go to a bookstore, and the store will have a few thousand copies of different books, but in many cases, they don't have the one that you want, so you have to place an order, give them your credit card, then go back in a few days or a week. They order the book in. This was the standard method of buying books, as you recall.

Bezos said, "What if I put together a deal with all the publishers, and a person who wanted a book could just

---

The *entrepreneur* is a person who sees an opportunity to serve people in some way with a product or service that they need, and then is able to bring this product or service to the customer at a cost that is lower than the customer is willing to pay.

---

order it online? They could order it on the computer, and it would be sent directly to their home by the publisher. Not only that, we could give them a discount, because we don't have to have a huge store. We don't have staff or delivery charges." It took off with an idea to serve people better-ER, fast-ER, cheap-ER, more conveniently.

These ideas are everywhere. So look at your world, and start off with yourself. Say, "What is it that I would want and need and be willing to pay for that would make my life or my work faster, better, easier, cheaper? Would this be something that other people would like?" The successful entrepreneurs are people who come up with an idea that lots of people want, and they get there "firstest" with the "mostest." They get into the marketplace first.

In entrepreneurship today, you can start with nothing. When I started my first business about twenty-five years ago, I had to lease offices for five years. I had to buy a large photocopier, which cost $30,000. I had to buy furniture. I had to hire and train staff. I had to have parking lots and stationery. It cost tens of thousands of dollars to start a very simple business.

Today I have several friends who will say, "Would you like to start a business? Come to my seminar and bring your laptop." In the course of that one-day seminar, they will show you how to start an online business, how to find a product or service that people want and need, how to market-test it, and then how to offer to sell it and have the money deposited in your bank account.

By the end of the day, with just a computer and instructions on how to start, build, and manage a business, you're actually generating sales and money, which is going into your bank account. This is something that anyone can learn.

There are skills that you have to have in our society. You have to be able to drive a car, you have to be able to use a computer, you have to be able to use an iPhone, and you have to be able to do a certain number of things that everybody considers to be automatic. They shake their head: why would you even say that? It's so obvious.

One skill you need, like reading, writing, and arithmetic, is entrepreneurship. Entrepreneurship is looking at your world as a world that's full of opportunities for creating wealth.

All financial success in our world is wealth creation. It's adding value of some kind, doing something. Jeff Bezos is a wonderful example, because his model is really very simple: You sell a book at a discount, and you deliver the book, and you make a profit. Then you do it again. That's basic entrepreneurship. It's not complicated. Large companies are companies that stumbled into something for which there was a huge market demand.

Sometimes I will ask my audiences how many of them work on straight commission. A certain number will raise their hand. I say, "Here's the fact: we all work on straight commission. We all get a percentage of the value that we create."

If you're in sales, you create wealth by finding a customer for the product or service that your company represents. You bring value to people. You bring the ER factor, if you like, and as a result, people are happy, they're satisfied, they buy your product, you make a profit, and you get a percentage of it.

The number-one reason businesses get into trouble is low sales. The number-one reason businesses succeed is high sales. Everything else is commentary. People will say, "We don't have enough money, we can't raise funds," but you can solve every single business problem by selling something. You have to sell something that people want and need and are willing to pay for right away. That is a learnable skill.

When I started off my career, the turning point in my life came after I had been struggling in door-to-door sales, hour after hour, up to 9:00 or 10:00 at night, knocking on doors, and selling a small knickknack. I wasn't making any sales. One day I went to the top sales guy in my company, and I asked him why he was making ten times as much as anybody else.

I was working from 8:00 in the morning until 9:00 or 10:00 at night five or six days a week. This guy was coming

---

"The number-one reason that businesses get into trouble is low sales. The number-one reason businesses succeed is high sales. Everything else is commentary."
—Brian Tracy

---

into work at 9:30 or 10:00, quitting work at 4:30, going to restaurants and nightclubs—a young guy like me, having a nice life. He said, "Show me your sales system, and I'll critique it for you." I said, "I don't have a sales system."

"What do you say when you talk to a customer?"

"I just say whatever I think at the moment."

"What do people say back?"

"They say, 'Let me think it over,' or 'I'm not interested,' or 'I'm not in the market,' or 'I can't afford it,' or 'I don't want it, I don't need it, can't use it,' and so on."

"No, no," he said. "That's not how you sell. If you're going to sell anything, first of all, you have to establish trust with the prospect."

There's 100 years of research that shows that no one will buy from you until they like you and trust you. So you establish trust. How do you establish trust? By being more concerned about helping the customer improve their life or work than about selling your product.

As soon as a customer feels that all you want to do is sell your product, it's over. They no longer have any interest in dealing with you.

So how do you build trust? How do you build rapport? How do you learn the customer's needs? How do you help the customer make a good choice? How do you make sure the customer gets the right product or service?

You do it by asking questions. Good salespeople, good businesspeople, good leaders ask a lot of questions so that they're very well-informed.

My friend said, "Here's how you sell," and he gave me a very basic sales process of asking questions and looking for opportunities to help people make good money decisions, answering their objections, and closing the sale.

It hit me like lightning, and still today I'm shocked by it: there's a system for everything. There's a sales system. There's a formula for success in any field. Napoleon Hill, the great motivational writer, said that the key to success is to find the success formula for that particular area of endeavor, and then start. It'd be the same as getting a recipe for a dish in the kitchen before you begin to cook.

For my first six months of selling, I just went out every single day. I got up at 6:00 or 7:00 in the morning and went out and knocked on doors, but I had no recipe. So I took a very simple recipe: get to know the customer, ask a lot of questions, find out what the customer wants and needs, and show them that my product or service could give it to them. As soon as I did that, my sales went up ten times.

Your job is to find the success formula. You do experimentation by trial and error, you ask people a lot of questions, you read and study, and you'll continually become better.

All success formulas are learnable. You can learn anything you need to learn. I am working with a group of business owners now who all want to become millionaires in the next three to five years. So I say, "OK, what do millionaires do starting from zero to become millionaires?"

When I started teaching, there were about one million millionaires in the world, most of whom were self-made. Today, there are more than ten million millionaires, most of whom are self-made. Eighty-seven percent of billionaires today are self-made. In other words, they started with nothing, and they learned a success formula. They developed it themselves, they worked with other people, and went through trial and error. They made all kinds of mistakes, and they finally got the formula.

Once they got the formula—like the McDonald's formula for fast food—they could roll it out, multiply it, and leverage it in every conceivable direction.

People—especially when they're just out of school and are very ambitious—wonder whether they should take the entrepreneurial path or the corporate path. How do you decide?

The foundational need for every human being is security. It goes back to psychologist Abraham Maslow. He found that until a person's need for survival and security, especially financial survival, are satisfied, they think about nothing else. In other words, if you run out of money, you think of nothing but money. You are obsessed with getting enough money to survive. So people come out of high school, and their first concern is security—earning enough money to be able to provide for themselves.

I've written a book on what I call the *E-factor*, the expediency factor: people always seek the fastest and easiest and most immediate way to get the things that they want right now, with little concern for long-term results or consequences. When people come out of school, they are offered a job, and it pays a salary, and they do it. It's simple: they say yes because they need to eat.

If you do something over and over again, you develop a habit. So these people develop the habit of going to work for wages. Different people have different levels of need.

Abraham Maslow's Top Discovery:
The foundational need for every human being is security.
Until a person's need for survival and security are satisfied,
they think about nothing else.

People want much more, so they will set much higher standards. Other people don't think about it.

In my courses, I ask, "What is the most valuable and important work that you do?" After people have thought about it for a while, I say that the answer is thinking—thinking in advance before you make a decision or take action. The most important word for success is *consequences*. What are the consequences of taking this particular action? The more time you spend thinking through in advance what you're going to do and what's likely to happen, the more likely you are to be successful.

Harvard did an incredible fifty-year study, conducted by Edward Banfield. They found that the most important factor that determines economic success is long-term thinking. Thinking ahead a year, two years, five years, ten years, twenty years.

Motivational speaker Denis Waitley used to say that successful people plant trees under which they will never sit. They're thinking into the next generation. They say the difference between a politician and a statesman is that a politician thinks about the next election, and a statesman thinks about the next generation.

Long-term thinking is about goals. If you sit down and think about your goals, you're much more likely to make the right decisions that have the right consequences that will in turn bring you the right kind of life.

The biggest enemy of success is the comfort zone. People quickly become accustomed to doing something and becoming habituated to it; as a result, they become comfortable. When they become comfortable, then they get into a rut. Another famous motivational speaker, Jim Rohn, used to say that the only difference between a rut and grave is the depth. You get into a rut, then you struggle and strive and fight to stay in that comfort zone.

There's an amazing fact about entrepreneurial influence: about 80 percent of entrepreneurs come from families where the mother or father was an entrepreneur. As a result, the person develops a belief system—that you can start and build a business. They learned it as children. It came through the skin. They saw their mother or father start with nothing, work hard, create a product or service, sell it and deliver it, and take good care of customers so that they bought again.

These people thought, "I can do that." It's automatic, so your success as an entrepreneur is largely determined by your beliefs. If, for example, you absolutely believe that you can start a business and become successful, you will, because there are millions of different products and services that people want and need, and they're changing, continually evolving all the time.

Eighty percent of the products and services that are being used today did not exist five years ago. Eighty percent of what we'll be using five years from now do not exist today. So the number of opportunities is beyond imagination. If you absolutely believe that you can start and build a successful business, you will make that belief a reality.

The great psychologist William James said belief creates the actual fact—if you have a strong enough belief. But if you don't, if you come from a limited background, if you had no entrepreneurs in your world and you associate with people who are going nowhere, then you'll go with them. You'll all go together. Entrepreneurship is very much a psychological thing.

Many entrepreneurs come from immigrants. Why is that? It's because they get here, and they don't know anybody, and they don't have any knowledge or skills, and they don't even know how to speak the language, so they have to provide for themselves. So they start selling something.

The essence of entrepreneurship is to find something that people want and need and are willing to pay for, and to sell it to them. Sell it to them in competition with other people who want to sell to them at the same time. Then get better and better at selling your product. You make the product better and better, so it's easier to sell.

You look at the examples today, and they're mind-shaking. The teenagers have this shorthand they use when they're sending messages; my favorite is SMH or "shaking my head." It's so simple. It's so obvious. It's so easy. Just shaking my head.

When immigrants came over and they didn't have anything, they bought old, used products and sold them on the street. The history of America and many other countries is people coming from the old country and selling stuff on the street. Some of these people now own massive department stores and conglomerates and factories, but they starting off selling one little product that was a little bit better-priced, better-quality, more convenient, and as a result they got better and better at it. They did more and more of it. They did it more and more easily. They made more and more money, and they expanded.

Entrepreneurship comes back to service. In my seminars—and I've given more than 5,000 seminars—I teach that you make a lot of money because you deserve it. Some say people who make a lot of money are rich, all they care about is money, and so on, but the word *deserve* comes from the Latin *deservire*, which means *to serve zealously*. People are successful from service, from serving other people.

You'll find that the most successful people are always thinking about how they can serve customers better than anyone else. They come up with a new food or a new product or a new service. The customers like it, and they buy it again.

When Steve Jobs came up with the iPhone a decade ago, the experts said, "It's for kids. It's for teenagers. It's just a plaything." They said it would never be successful.

In the year after the iPhone was released, BlackBerry had 49 percent of the world business market in cell phones. The top people at BlackBerry said, "The iPhone is a toy. We are so far ahead that we're going to reduce our research and development expenditures by 50 percent, because we don't need to improve or change our phone at all." Five years later they were bankrupt.

People are successful from service,
from serving other people.

As of 2017, Apple had sold about 800 million iPhones. Here's another thing: they did a survey of Apple iPhone owners a couple of months ago, and asked, "Do you intend to purchase another iPhone in the future?" Ninety percent said yes.

A few years ago, people said, "Apple's finished. They've hit their peak. Now it's time to sell and buy something else." The smart money, like Warren Buffett, kept buying Apple. Why? Because they looked at the numbers, and the numbers said that 90 percent of purchasers were going to purchase another. What does Apple do with their prices? They raise them every year. The prices are higher and higher, so Apple's profits are higher and higher.

Apple stock is the most valuable stock in the world. It's the most phenomenal thing, and why? It's because they're always looking for ways to add features and benefits to the phone that make it more attractive than it was before.

As for choosing corporate work over entrepreneurship, everything in business is knowledge and skill: knowing how to do it and then applying it. Management expert Peter Drucker said that 80 percent of businesses fail within the first two to four years. But 80–90 percent of businesses started by people with business experience succeed.

So if you are going to have your own business, the first thing you need to learn is how to do business: how to market, how to sell, how to produce products, how to take care of customers, and so on. Unless you're going to spend your whole life at it, you can only do this by working for another company.

We talk about going to work for corporations. Most of our readers don't have the opportunity to work for companies and earn $100,000 or $150,000 a year. The average salary in the United States today is about $22,000 a year. Family income is $50,000, and people have to eat every day, three times a day. Unless you've gone to an excellent school and you come from a great family with tremendous connections, you just don't have the luxury to do otherwise.

If you're highly skilled and you go to work for a high-tech company, you could earn a lot of money, but 80 to 90 percent of us are going to have to start at the bottom. We have to get experience, so the first thing you do is get experience. Go to work for someone. Work really hard and get really good at the job. Get promoted until you finally reach the point where you break through: the point of saying, "I don't need to do this for someone else. I can do it for myself."

It takes three, four, five, seven years' experience. So unless you're desperate, unless you have to find something that you can sell and earn a profit from right away, the best thing is go to work for another company. You learn to go to work, to be on time, to complete the job, to finish up afterwards, to be nice to your boss, to be polite to your customers, and so on. These are things you cannot learn anywhere else.

Something like 50 percent of Americans start their career by going to work for McDonald's. McDonald's is the most popular entry-level position in the United States and in many other countries as well, because you learn all the essential skills.

Whom am I going to hire? Somebody who sits in the back and drinks coffee and smokes cigarettes, arrives at the last minute, goes home at the first minute, and so on? Or do you hire somebody who comes in early, works hard, stays later, and is constantly upgrading their skills? If you're an employer with half a brain, you're going to hire the person who's going to help you take care of your customers better than anyone else.

It's true that even corporations are wanting to become more entrepreneurial—the term is *intrapreneurial.* In fact, I created a program on internal innovation—being an intrapreneur, finding ways within the company to do the job faster, better, cheaper, and easier, and going back to creating value. It's about looking for ways to give your company more value than you gave them before, or than other people are giving them.

You can actually achieve all of your goals within an established company if you constantly get better at what you do and help the company to take care of its customers.

Intrapreneur: An employee who looks for ways within the company to do the job faster, better, cheaper and easier, and going back to creating value.

Here's another thing. Drucker said that most people are not suited for entrepreneurship. Don't write off entrepreneurship, but most people are suited to specializing: doing a particular job really well, getting better and better at that job, and then working in cooperation with other people who also do what they do well.

A company is made up of people who have a small number of strengths and an enormous number of weaknesses. One of my favorite lines from Drucker is that the purpose of an organization is to emphasize strengths and to make weaknesses irrelevant: to bring out the strengths in the best people, and to make weaknesses irrelevant by having somebody else do that job.

Some of the most productive and valuable people in our society are people who work within a company all their lives, but they get very good at doing what they're doing, and they are *intra*-preneurs. They're constantly seeking faster, better, cheaper, easier ways to help the company to achieve its goals. So you can do that, and you can achieve all your financial goals.

Other people are more oriented toward individuality: they like being their own boss. It's a different route to success, but they are psychologically designed for it, and they love entrepreneurship.

Most entrepreneurs, as I've found in my research, earn less than they would if they worked for wages. But there are psychological benefits: entrepreneurs will settle for less money so they can be their own boss. They have freedom, they have independence, they have choice.

The biggest mistake that entrepreneurs make is that they slip into a comfort zone shortly after starting their business, and they just coast. They don't get any better. They *don't* constantly upgrade their skills or look for newer, better, faster, cheaper ways to do their work. They just become comfortable. That's the great tragedy.

It's the 80/20 rule: 20 percent of people are constantly working to get better at what they're doing, and 80 percent coast. The great tragedy with coasting is you can only do it in one direction.

Some people ask if the push toward automation is going to eliminate many traditional jobs and force people into entrepreneurship. If you look at current statistics today, you see three groups of people: the lower paid, the middle paid, and the upper paid. These are just employees. They're not executives or company owners. There's an average of about three million job openings in each of those categories.

If you speak to company owners and managers, they will tell you that they cannot find good people, or talented people. Although people say, "Automation is going to eliminate all of these jobs, and we won't be able to get jobs," it's exactly the opposite, and it's been the opposite for 200 years.

Do you know that at the turn of the twentieth century, 80 to 90 percent of American workers worked on the farm? Today about one percent work on the farm, but we produce twenty times the food that we produced 100 years ago. It's because farm equipment and food production are so modern. They pour out a cornucopia of food.

At the turn of the twentieth century, 80 to 90 percent of Americans worked on the farm. Today about one percent work on the farm, but we produce twenty times the food that we produced 100 years ago.

We have the lowest-priced and highest-quality food in the history of the world.

This idea that the jobs will be lost because of automation is wrong. Here's what I found: boring jobs are automated, so these jobs, being in production lines and standing in a row all day long, earning minimum wage, are eliminated. They're automated.

Factories can do them, so these people can do more intellectually demanding work. They do more work interacting with other people, creative work, customer-service work. They're doing things that are more enjoyable and more interactive. For most people, their greatest enjoyment in working is interacting with others.

What people want in a job is to have a good time with their coworkers. They want to work well, be acknowledged, get better in their field, get promoted, and be admired by their coworkers. This is what makes people happy, and you can't do that if you're working on a production line. Therefore every time a work process is automated, more working talent is freed up to do things that are much more enjoyable and pay more.

The first major turning point in my life was when I was working as a laborer, living in a small, one-bedroom apartment with a foldout bed and a little kitchen in the middle of the winter, earning just enough money to get up at 5:00 in the morning, take three buses to work, finish work at 5:30 or 6:00 at night, and take two or three buses home. I didn't have enough money to go out and socialize, so I stayed in my little apartment.

One evening I realized that I was responsible for my own life. This was my life—sitting here in this little apartment with little money, cold as blazes in the middle of a very cold winter. Nothing was going to get any better unless *I* got better. I was responsible, and I still remember this almost like a light bulb flashing in my face.

From that moment on, my life changed. It didn't change overnight. I didn't suddenly leap a building with a single bound, but from that point on, I realized that I was responsible.

Look at Stephen Covey's book *The Seven Habits of Highly Successful People*. First chapter: take charge of your life, accept responsibility. Look at Jack Canfield's book *The Success Principles*. First chapter: accept responsibility, take charge of your life. In my books, I always talk about the importance of accepting responsibility and taking charge of your life.

Before that happens in your life, nothing happens. You just go along with the crowd, you do an average job, you don't make any progress, you think all of your problems are caused by someone else. The most popular choice here is your parents. Your parents did or didn't do certain things that led you to where you are today. After that it's your boss, and your spouse, and your siblings, and things like that.

Eighty percent of people go through their entire lives blaming their problems on something outside themselves. Well, if you give up your responsibility, you give up your power. If you give up your power, you never make any changes. You just keep going along as you were before, because you're not responsible. If you get fired, it was the boss's fault. If you're not making very much money, it's the economy, it's the politicians.

Many years ago motivational speaker Earl Nightingale said that each person chooses their own income at every stage of their life. They choose their income by what they do and what they fail to do. If they don't set goals and upgrade their skills and work continually to get better at what they do, then their income is flat. They make very little progress.

If you want to deserve more money, then you have to deserve it by serving other people at a better and higher level. You have to start a little earlier, work a little harder, and stay a little later. You cannot be successful simply by sitting there and demanding that someone else increase your income.

You see people that are protesting and demonstrating for higher incomes. If you want a higher income, be more productive. What they're saying is "I want more money, but I do not want to change anything I'm doing, and I don't want to be more productive."

I was watching one of those demonstrations recently, and the newscasters were interviewing someone in the crowd. The person said, "I'm thirty-four years old, and I'm only earning minimum wage." You're thirty-four years

> "Each person chooses their own income at
> every stage of their life." —Earl Nightingale

old. When did you take your first job? "When I was seven-teen or eighteen."

So after almost twenty years in one of the most afflu-ent countries in the history of the world, with thousands of learning institutions and courses on every conceivable subject available online at almost no price or free, you have made no progress at all. After twenty years, you're still earning minimum wage. You should not be announc-ing it to the press. You should be embarrassed. You should put a bag over your head, because after twenty years, you're still so unproductive that you're complaining and crying, and it's always someone else. It's the boss. It's the company. It's the economy.

I've learned that each person is responsible for their own income. Each person writes their own check, so, how-ever much you're earning today, that's the amount you have decided to earn.

I will often ask my audiences, "What is your most valu-able financial asset?" There will usually be silence. I will say, "When I first heard this question, I didn't know the answer either. Then I found out that your most valuable financial asset is your earning ability." It's your ability to earn money. It's your ability to get results that people will pay you for. If you want to increase your earning ability, you have to work on yourself so that you can get more and better results faster so that people will willingly pay you more. People will try to drag you from wherever you're working today and pay you more money. If you become more productive at your work, they'll pay you even more because they don't want you to leave.

A very good friend of mine applied for a job as a salesman at IBM when he was in school. They interviewed him two, three, four times, and eventually they turned him down. They said, "We decided not to hire you at this time, but keep in touch with us in case something opens up."

So he did. He finished school, went out and got a job, and continued to work on himself and to read and upgrade his skills. He went into sales, and he became successful as a salesperson. Once a month, he would send a report to the hiring manager at IBM, and he did this for about two years.

At the end of two years, he called them up at IBM, and they brought him in. They said, "We've decided to offer you a job." He was ecstatic. That had been his goal for a long time. He went to work for IBM, and he got fabulous training. He'd been earning maybe $25,000 a year. IBM started him at $50,000. Within a couple of years, he was at $100,000; within five years, at $150,000, and so on.

After he was really secure at IBM, he asked them, "Why didn't you hire me when you first spoke to me? What was wrong with me?" They said, "We never hire anybody when we first speak to them. We tell them we're interested and tell them to keep in touch with us, and then we watch to see what they do. If they just quit and go out and get a Joe job, that's obviously not a person we want at IBM."

My friend said, "But you pay so well, starting off at a great salary, and then keep raising the salary. Why do you do that?" They said, "Because we train you; we upgrade your skills. By upgrading your skills, we enable you to make more and better sales and become more profitable. We make you more and more valuable to the company, so we're going to pay you more and more because we don't want you to go away."

If you go to work for a good company, and you do a really good job, you become an asset to that company. You become an incredible value, and they don't want to lose you.

In my company, every year I used to do what I called a *preemptive increase*. I would go to a staff member and say, "You are doing a really good job, and I'd like to give you more money, because I really appreciate the job that you're doing and I don't want you to go anywhere else. Would that be OK?"

Surprise, surprise—100 percent of my staff members agreed that they would take more money, but nobody ever had to ask me for an increase. I was running a small business, thirty people, but nobody ever had to come and say, "Can I have an increase?" because they all knew if they did a good job, I would come around like a hummingbird visiting flowers.

I'd say, "I want to pay you more money because you're doing such a good job. I don't want you to go anywhere else. I really appreciate you." For decades, everybody in my company was happy. They smiled, they laughed, they got along well with other people, they did their jobs well, and they knew that if they did a good job, they were going to get more money. That's the way our world works.

You don't ever have to worry about getting more money. You focus on the one thing you can control, which is the quality and quantity of your work. If you focus on the quality and quantity of your work, the money will come automatically.

I'm often asked about the personal qualities of successful entrepreneurs. For thirty or forty years I have studied the characteristics, qualities, behavior of such people; Harvard has studied them also. What is it that enables a person to be successful? They've come up with one conclusion.

Number one, more important than anything else, is *ambition*. That accounts for 80 percent or more of success. If a person is ambitious enough, is driven enough, is determined enough to be successful, nothing will stop them.

There was an interesting story about the difference between the American attitude and the European attitude. In the United States, if you start a business and you go broke, you can start a new business the next day. In Europe, if you start a business and you go broke, you're looked down upon as though you have committed some awful crime. It's a terrible thing to lose money if you go out of business. But in the US, we admire it, we respect it.

Think about Bill Gates or Warren Buffett: these are the richest people in history. In America, you never hear them criticized. In Europe, wealthy people are criticized and sneered at and resented and accused of all kinds of things. Here, people who are wealthy and successful, like

---

The number one quality of a successful entrepreneur is
ambition.

Jeff Bezos—nobody criticizes them. People admire them. They respect them. They fantasize, "Maybe I can be like that. My kids could be like that."

Someone once asked, "Why are the people in Europe content to live in a welfare system, have lower wages, and have the government take care of almost everything for them from cradle to grave, whereas in the US, everybody is entrepreneurial?" The reply was, "The US is made up of people who left, and Europe is made up of people who stayed." In other words, no ambition.

It takes ambition to pack up and leave everything behind and maybe never see your friends and family again, and to go to a new country with no knowledge or skills or contacts and to build a life, not only for yourself, but for your children and your children's children. This is long-term thinking: "I may not do a lot in my life. I may work as a laborer or a factory worker, but my children can go to school and go to college and become doctors and lawyers."

They're willing to invest twenty or thirty years of their lives for the next generation. So ambition is the most important quality.

The second turning point in my life was when I discovered goals. It was like dying and going to heaven. I was living on the floor of a small room that a friend of mine had, and it was hot outside, so I stayed inside, where there was air-conditioning. I read an article that said if you want to be successful, you have to have goals. You have to know what you want. So I found a scrap of paper and turned it over. It was blank.

I said, "OK, my goals are . . ." and I wrote down ten goals. Within thirty days, my life had changed completely. I found that if you have clear, written goals that you want to accomplish, you increase the likelihood of achieving those goals by about ten times.

You can't hit a target that you can't see, so you write down your goals, and then you make a list of everything that you can think of that you could do to achieve the goal. Then you organize the list by priority and sequence. What would you do first? What would you do second? Then you go to work on it.

Every single day, you get up and work on your most important goal. Soon—sometimes overnight—your life begins to develop a certain momentum. You start to move faster towards your goals. You've heard about the Law of Attraction. A written goal activates your powers of attraction: it attracts people, circumstances, ideas, insights, all kinds of things into your life.

Do you know that only 3 percent of adults have written goals? I learned this from Earl Nightingale many years ago. The other 97 percent have wishes and hopes and dreams and fantasies, but they don't have any goals. Three percent have goals, and these 3 percent earn on average ten times as much as people without written goals.

It has nothing to do with intelligence or education or background or opportunity. When you have a written goal, you focus your mind, you channel your mental abilities and energies, and you accomplish vastly more.

Imagine going to a new city in a new country. You have no roadmap and no road signs, and you try to get somewhere. You could drive around in circles forever without very clear, written goals and plans.

Wealthy people decide to become wealthy. One of the turning points in life is to make a decision to become wealthy in business. Then you realize that you can't become wealthy working for an average wage. Average wage is about $22 an hour in the United States, and much less for an enormous number of people.

So you make a decision that you're going to become financially independent. Then the only question you ask is, how? How do I become financially independent? What are the channels that are open to me?

It's appropriate at this time to bring up the third turning point in my life. I found that you can learn anything you need to learn to achieve any goal you can set for yourself by doing lots and lots and lots of work with company owners and entrepreneurs. The biggest single problem has always been fear of rejection, fear of failure.

If you want to earn money, you have to create wealth, and you can create wealth by bringing a product from one place to another place and charging more for it. It's called *arbitrage*. The entire world of trade is based on arbitrage, whether it's bringing a peppercorn from the Far East to Europe or silk from China along the Silk Road. It's bringing stuff from one place where it has a lower value and bringing it to a place where people will pay more for it.

Arbitrage: Creating wealth by bringing a product from one place to another place and charging more for it.

You can learn anything you need to learn. People say, "I can't be an entrepreneur because I don't like to sell."

So I ask, "Can you drive a car?" They say yes.

"Do you remember how you felt when you drove your first car?" I ask. They say yes.

"How did you feel?"

"Really nervous, really scared or shaking," they say. "The person who was trying to teach me to drive was shouting at me, and I was going all over the road."

"How about today?" I say. "Today you can get in a car, and you can drive all day long, and not even think about it. It's the same with any skill. Same with typing, same with anything else. You can learn the skill. You can learn the skill of driving. You can learn the skill of selling."

Everyone is in sales. Everyone is trying to persuade other people to cooperate with them in some way. Either you're active in your world or you're passive. If you're active, you try to make things happen. If you're passive, you sit there and you wait and expect other people to make decisions for you.

People are not good at sales because they have not been taught how to sell. When I changed my career, I had learned how to sell by going out and knocking on doors. I began to read every book and listen to audio programs and go to seminars on the subject. I became very successful in sales in every company and with every product or service I worked in.

Then I began to teach other people. I had people come to me in their twenties. These people were struggling. They had no money, they were desperate, they were frustrated, but the only way they could earn any money was to sell my product, so I taught them how to sell my product.

Many of these people today are millionaires and multi-millionaires. Once they learned how to sell, they overcame their fear of it, because the more you learn how to do something, the less fear you have. Eventually you reach the point where you have no fear at all. Then you set the bar higher, and you set bigger standards and you have bigger goals.

One friend of mine owns twelve companies now. The man is worth millions and millions of dollars, and he said, "It all started when you taught me how to sell. After that, I became successful at it. I was never afraid of anything." So you can overcome your fear of selling just by doing it.

First of all, take skills. I worked with a multibillion-dollar Fortune 500 company. This company generated millions of dollars in sales each year. It's the number-one company of its kind in the world today. They invited me to speak to their top salespeople in Las Vegas at their annual convention. They had 4,000 salespeople, and they took the top 20 percent—800 salespeople—to Las Vegas. They wined and dined them and took them to clubs and dinners and restaurants.

I asked the senior executive of sales, "These people are positive, they're happy, and they're high-energy. Where do you get them?" He said, "We hire them straight out of school. If they have demonstrated that they can get good grades, it means that they can learn what they need to learn. Most of them come terrified of the idea of selling. We say, 'Don't worry. We'll simply show you our system, like a recipe. We'll send you out with one of our experienced people, and they'll put you through the recipe and give you some feedback until you feel confident enough to do it yourself.'"

These people go out, generate millions of dollars of sales each year, and make this company one of the most successful companies in history in its field. Before they started, they could not sell anything. They simply learned how to do it.

It's the same thing with IBM. IBM hires on the basis of a positive personality. You have a good personality and get good grades, which means you're ambitious; you're hard-working. Can you sell? No. You're probably terrified of selling.

So they say, "Don't worry. We'll simply teach you the recipe." They teach the recipe. And what happens? At one time IBM had 82 percent of the world computer market. IBM salespeople were rated as the best salespeople in the high-tech world. But none of them could sell before they started.

Don't allow yourself to be held back as an entrepreneur because you're a little nervous about selling and a little fearful of rejection. That's OK. Everybody starts off that way; it's the same as driving a car. Once you have learned it, soon you'll reach the point where you have no nerves at all. You're just a normal, natural, friendly, and persuasive person trying to help people to improve their life and work.

Imagine: the great majority of people remain poor and at low-level jobs because they fear rejection. It's fear that holds them back. I learned this right at the beginning of my speaking: that fear of failure and rejection account for about 95 to 98 percent of all failure. It's not failure that holds you back; it's *fear* of failure. It's thinking about failure: "What would happen if I fail?"

I used to joke with my audience. I would say, "When they told me I was coming here today, they told me I would be speaking to a roomful of professional failures. They told me these people fail, have failed so many times, they've failed over and over again. They're complete failures."

At first the audience would react to that in a negative way, and then I would say, "Isn't that true? How many times have you failed, made mistakes, tried things, picked yourself up, just kept on going? Is anybody here wounded, bleeding, having lost a limb, or anything else?" Then they would start to laugh.

Every time I gave that little diatribe, they'd react negatively, and then they'd realize, "Of course. I've failed so many times." I'd say, "You're still here, and you're still going. Isn't all your success a result of having failed in the past and learned?" They'd all nod. So the whole audience is kind of happy that they have been designated as professional failures. Without the failure, there's no success.

So you need ambition. You have very clear goals for being successful. There is another quality you need. I call these the bookends of success. The second quality is, you never quit. You make a decision in advance that you will never give up. You decide, "All right, I am going to be successful as an entrepreneur, as a business owner."

On *The David Susskind Show*, a popular interview show some years ago, they had four self-made millionaires. They'd all become millionaires before the age of twenty-five. Just before the break, the interviewer asked them, "How many different businesses did you try before you became a millionaire?"

At the break, they sat down and calculated, and they came back with an average of seventeen. They had failed or semi-failed or gone broke or almost broke sixteen times, and on the seventeenth one they struck gold.

The rest of the conversation was about this: did they actually fail? The answer was no. They just learned. What they learned in the first sixteen runs was what made number seventeen possible. There's no such thing as failure. There's only feedback. Difficulties comes not to obstruct but to instruct. Therefore every single problem or difficulty contains one or more lessons.

The average person thinks about the loss, the pain, the penalty, how much time and money they invested and lost it all. The superior person says, "What did I learn from this?"

I did the same thing with my children. When they made a mistake, I'd ask, "What did you learn?" I'd force them to focus on what they learned. They'd say, "I learned this, and I'm not going to do this anymore." I'd say, "Great. You just scrunch it up and throw it away. Keep the lesson and let the rest go."

A successful entrepreneurial multimillionaire might take the dictionary, cut out the word *barrier*, and burn it in an ashtray. We make lots of mistakes. We lose lots of money. We try all kinds of things. We have many learning experiences, but we never fail. The word *failure* does not exist in this organization.

You must make that decision in advance: *I will never quit. I will never quit.* If this doesn't work, something else will work, and all you focus on is what you learned. What did I learn from this experience that will help me in the future?

I have a good friend who started off selling on the street. Then, with friends of his, he started a business. They worked on this business for three or four years, and it failed. They lost all their time and money and went broke. He had to move back in with his mother. (I've done the same thing, by the way. I went through a major financial reversal, spent a lot of time and money, and lost both.)

My friend was sitting there, depressed. A friend of his asked, "What did you learn?" He said, "I learned this, and I learned that." His friend said, "Write it down." So he got a spiral notebook, and he divided it up into categories.

A second quality of a successful entrepreneur:
They make this decision in advance:
I will never quit. I will never quit.

He took the spiral notebook and wrote, "What did I learn about people?" Next page: "What did I learn about money?" Next page: "What did I learn about customers?" Next page: "What did I learn about finances?" Next page: "What did I learn about business partnerships?"

He wrote down several categories, and he wrote down every lesson he learned in each of these categories. That became his bible. He started another business, as people do; they bounce back. He took that notebook as his reference work, and he said, "All right. What did I learn about people and partners and money and customers and sales last time?"

He would refer back to his book, and he became successful. Of course he went through some ups and downs, but he became more and more successful. By the age of fifty, he was a multimillionaire. He retired to Palm Springs, where he plays golf every day. He's wealthy and never has to work again.

He told me the reason for his success was that he wrote down the lessons. I did the same thing. I'd go back to those lessons every time I've gotten into a business situation that was similar; I'd read the lessons. It's priceless. You can almost guarantee your success if you extract the lessons.

But if you don't write down what you've learned, the chances are that you will repeat them and you'll gain nothing from them. You'll become resentful. You'll blame other people, and so on. So just write it down.

In my company, when my staff would have a problem, I would say, "OK, stuff happens. Problems happen. What did you learn?"

One of the great lessons for entrepreneurs is to accept that you cannot change a past event. If something happens, and it doesn't work out, it's happened. The only thing you can do is learn from it. You don't become angry, you don't blame, you don't resent, you don't sulk, you don't see yourself as a victim. You say, "It's unfortunate that this has happened, but the only thing I can do is learn from it and throw the rest away." This attitude enables you to see insights and possibilities that you would have never seen if you were busy being angry or resentful.

There is a story about Winston Churchill. It was at Harrow, the preparatory school that he had gone to. He went back at the end of his career, and one of the students asked him what was the most important lesson that he ever learned, and it was exactly what you said. He stood up, and he said, "Never give up. Never, never give up, except in situations of morals and values. Never give up," and he sat back down again.

To sum up, you become wealthy based on your own efforts by deciding exactly what you want, writing it down, making a plan, going to work on it, and working on it until you are successful. I wrote a book a couple of years ago, and they didn't pick the title, but my title was *Get Going and Keep Going*. The key to success: get going and keep

---

Winston Churchill's Most Important Lesson:
"Never give up. Never, never give up, except in
situations of morals and values. Never give up."

going. Decide exactly what you want and get started, and then never give up until you are successful.

If you make that decision in advance, you actually program yourself so that you put a kind of spring inside your psyche telling you that you may have setbacks and reversals that cause unhappiness and disappointment, but you just bounce back. You just keep bouncing back. You never, never stop. You go like the Energizer Bunny. You just keep going until you succeed.

Here's another discovery. Almost everybody who succeeds greatly does it in an area that is completely different from where they started off. They started off going in one direction, and they had reversal after reversal and then finally picked up their head and were hugely successful. It was very different from where they started, very different from what they envisioned. The reason they succeeded is that they just never gave up.

2

Myths of Modern Entrepreneurship

Before we go on, I want to talk about some of the biggest myths about modern entrepreneurship.

Myths of Modern Entrepreneurship
1. Ninety-five percent of all businesses fail within the first five years.
2. You have to have venture capitalists to fund a start-up.
3. If your product or service is good, you'll be successful.
4. To be a successful entrepreneur, you need to invent something novel and groundbreaking
5. Most entrepreneurs are wild risk takers.
6. Most entrepreneurs are financially successful.

7. Entrepreneurs are born, not made.
8. All entrepreneurs want to be rich.
9. Entrepreneurs have no personal lives.

Myth 1: Ninety-five percent of all businesses fail within the first five years.

I've worked with thousands of business owners all over the world. Over and over again, I have found that *preparation is the key to success*. It's taking the time to carefully examine every detail of the business before you get into it.

Entrepreneurs tend to be impulsive and impatient, which is why they take risks and start businesses, but they have to hold themselves back. It's like holding back a horse. They have to take the time and go meticulously through every aspect of the business. Before they do, they need to ask themselves three questions.

THREE QUESTIONS YOU NEED TO ASK BEFORE YOU START A BUSINESS

1. *Is there a market for your product or service?*
2. *Is your market large enough?*
3. *Is your market concentrated enough?*

1. There may be a relative or friend of yours who thinks your product or service is a great idea, but is there a market for it? There may be a tiny market. There may be one person. Will people actually give you money for the product?

2. Is your market large enough? Large enough, that is, that you can make a profitable business out of it?

3. Is your market concentrated enough so that you can focus in on it and sell enough of your product while meeting the costs of advertising, promotion, distribution, and so on?

The biggest mistake that people make is coming up with a product or service for which there is no substantial market. It seems like a good idea at the time, but you have to do your preparation. What is your proof that the market exists?

In modern business today, we have what is called *proof of concept*. If you have an idea, that's a concept. It's not a truth. How do you prove that this concept is true?

This is the only proof that there is a market: people give you money for it. How many customers can you get who will actually give you checks for your product or service when it isn't available in the market?

People may say, "It's a great idea. You produce the product, you bring it out, and you'll be really successful."

"Good. Would you give me a deposit check?"

"Hold on."

You need a business plan, which forces you to think through every aspect of the business. Is there a market? Is the market large enough? How do you reach the mar-

---

This is the only proof that there is a market for your product or service: people give you money for it.

ket? How much will the market pay for the product? Who's the competition for what you're selling? What are other companies doing now that's different from what you're offering, and so on?

Then you have to get the pricing and the costing and the delivery. You have to tell how much it's going to cost to sell, how much to produce, to distribute. How much are you going to have to pay people to sell the product?

Sometimes the problem is with defects or broken items: you have to take them back. Sometimes the problem is the delivery cost. I worked with a company that had a great idea. They figured that the product was so good that people would buy it automatically, but they found that the total selling cost was about 40 percent. A 40 percent selling cost made it impossible to even think of bringing this kind of product to the market.

I got into a multimillion-dollar investment deal. It was presented to me by my partner, who wrote it all out. It looked great, and I invested a lot of money in it. It was a real-estate development product that was going to take about two years from inception—acquisition of the land— to being fully occupied and generating revenues.

My friend was either not smart or not honest. He did not include carrying costs, interest costs, which were from 6 to 8 percent per annum on the amount invested in both the property and the construction. That amounted to an enormous amount of money. By the time we reached the peak of development, with no revenue, we were running $50,000 a month, which almost bankrupted us, because these costs had not been included.

How long will it take before you break even and generate revenues, and how long will it take before you'll get your money back? They hadn't thought about that, or about the interest charges. It was not even included in the business projections.

So think it through. When I was in my twenties, I learned a great rule, which has stood me in good stead all my life: *think on paper*. Write everything down. Write it down so that an objective and even a critical, skeptical third party can question you on every single principle. Never assume anything when you're starting or building a business. Check and double-check. Get the numbers and write them down.

I was getting into this deal. I put it all together. My friends took the plan, came back to me, and said, "You didn't include these numbers. You didn't include these costs. You didn't include this interest. Here's what it would look like if you counted all these costs."

Here's the rule: everything takes three times as long and costs twice as much. I learned that, again, early in my career. I have taught it to thousands of business owners, entrepreneurs, start-up people, and people have come back to me over and over again. They said, "I thought I was going to beat that number. I didn't like that number. I kind of ignored it, but it was always true year after year. It costs twice as much and takes three times as long."

If you think you're going to break even in three months, you're probably going to break even in nine months. If you think something is going to cost X, it's going to cost 2X, so build that into your calculations. If it doesn't, you can consider yourself very fortunate.

Preparation is the mark of the professional. You never take anything for granted. You never assume anything. You check and you double-check every number and every fact. You get proof of concept. You get outside proof. Many companies will hire an outside company to come in, take all of their numbers, analyze them, and come back with the truth. The truth is your best friend.

I worked with a friend who started off with nothing, and now he's very wealthy. He was going into this business. He had the cash because he was quite successful, and the market opportunity seemed good. So he and two people in his office embarked on gathering research, checking and double-checking, speaking to people in the industry, and so on. They spent six months doing this. At the end of it, they came back and said, "Nope, it's not a good deal."

There's a wonderful little story about Warren Buffett, currently the fourth-richest man in the world. He was out playing golf, and his companion said, "Warren, I'll bet you $1,000 you can't put the ball on the green from the tee off." Buffett looked at the green, and he looked at the tee off, and he said, "No. I'm not going to do it. It's not a good bet."

His companion said, "Come on, Warren, $1,000 to you is like pocket change. It's nothing to you." Buffett said, "Foolish in small things, foolish in big things. I'm not going to do it. It's a foolish bet."

You have to have that same attitude. Foolish in small things, foolish in big things. If you're willing to do silly things with small amounts of money, you are inevitably going to do really dumb things with large amounts of money.

One of my mentors, who started with nothing and built a fortune of $900 million, told me, "Brian, it's always easier to get into something than to get out of it. The time to do all of your due diligence and all of your careful thinking is before you invest time and money. You may have to invest time; that's inevitable. You may have even have to invest small amounts of money to check, to get proof of concept, but the time to do your main investigation is before you get in, because it's always harder to get out than to get in."

My favorite words in business are *due diligence*. Check and double-check everything. The biggest, costliest mistakes that I've made, which can wipe out years of hard work and savings, are not to do your due diligence, not to do your checking, not to do your preparation. That's the starting point.

Here's another thing: always be prepared to replace financial equity, capital, with sweat equity. In other words, be prepared to put in the time and invest the necessary hours to do your research and to get your information rather than putting in money. The time is retrievable, but the money is not, and anyway it's not the money that you invest in a business. It's the amount of time of your life it's taken you to accumulate that money in the first place.

Brian Tracy's favorite two words in business: *due diligence*.
This means to check and double check everything.

You are losing your time, which is a piece of your life, plus you're losing the money by not doing proper research. That would save more than 90 percent of the problems people have with their business.

I get requests for money to invest every week, sometimes two or three times a week. They're sort of like hard-luck stories. "I have this great business idea, but nobody will give me any money to start. I have this great business concept, but I can't find anybody who will give me any money. Banks won't lend me any money. Nobody will lend me any money."

I try to be as gentle as possible, but I point out that if you are a full-fledged adult, and you have no money to invest in your business, then you are not a good investment. If you've lived your life twenty or thirty years, and you are broke, and you have to go to someone else hat in hand to get enough money to promote your business concept, you are not a safe investment. You're too dangerous.

Most people who will lend money will go in on a hand-in-hand basis: I'll put in my money, you put in yours. If you go to a bank to borrow money—which I did at one time years ago—they want to know that you have hurting money, all your savings and your investments and assets, in the deal.

I was astonished to learn that in order to lend money to a new or even an existing business, banks want to be covered five times. My banker told me this: "We want five times cost collateralization. If you want to borrow $10,000 from us, we want you to demonstrate to us that you have $50,000 in different reserves, cars, homes, savings accounts, insurance policies, and so on, that you can draw on to pay the money back." Five times. I couldn't believe it. After you have a two-year history of profits, they will start to cut back gently on the amount of coverage that they require.

Banks are not in the business of losing money. Banks are in the business of making good loans. Good loans are loans that will be paid back no matter what happens to your business or your collateral. When you are trying to borrow money, your job is to convince them that you really don't need it, that you have lots of money, but you need or want the loan to enable you to grow faster.

Myth 2: You have to have venture capitalists to fund a start-up.

Some people see venture capitalists as the answer, but ninety-nine out of 100 applications to venture capitalists are thrown in the wastebasket. That's why you need to get your elevator pitch—to be able to summarize the soundness of your investment within the length of time it takes an elevator to go up or down eight floors.

If you watch a program like *Shark Tank*, you see that the primary reason candidates are turned down is lack of sales. The investors do not believe you're going to get enough sales to be successful as a business. You're not going to make the sales, or the sales are not going to be profitable enough. On *Shark Tank*, you're asking for an enormous amount of money for 10 percent of the business, but you have not convinced them. And you haven't convinced anyone else, because you've been in business for two or three years and you've made almost no sales at all.

There's lots of capital, lots of money available. The money flows like a river to people who can demonstrate that they can pay it back plus a profit. Therefore your job is not to find a clever argument for people to give you money. Your job is to show that you can generate sales well in excess of costs. You have to persuade that you have a great opportunity here, and with a little bit of extra capital, you could capitalize on this opportunity quickly.

In Silicon Valley, you can struggle an enormous amount to get a little bit of money and maybe not even that—most of it will be friends and family—to start a business and to generate a profit. Sometimes it will take you five to seven years of hard work starting from nothing to do this. Then your business is successful, and you can sell it, and you make a lot of money for yourself and for the people who trusted you. After that, they line up to give you money. The money is there like a river. Just prove to me that you'll pay it back.

People are not in the business of losing money. They're not in the business of taking risks. People think the role of the entrepreneur is to take risks, but taking risks is not the role of the entrepreneur. The role of the entrepreneur is to mitigate risk, to alleviate risk, to eliminate risk. The money is there as long as you can demonstrate that you can sell enough of your product or service to pay the money back and substantially more.

Most businesses today are funded by the three F's: family, friends, and fools. It's your money, it's your

---

The money flows like a river to people who can
demonstrate that they can pay it back plus a profit.

---

family's money, it's your friends' money, and it's fools'
money, because a high percentage of new enterprises
fail over time.

If it's a brand-new product or service, the failure rate
is extraordinary. Usually it's because the person has no
experience. They've never brought a product or service
like this to market.

I started my business by bootstrapping. This is also
how scores of entrepreneurs started. It's actually very
simple. You get an idea for a product or service, you go
out, you sell it, and you make a profit. You take that profit,
you turn it back into the business, you produce and sell a
product or service, and you make another profit. Then you
do it again.

This may take months or years, but it's far better to go
into your business with the minimum amount of money
to survive than it is to go in with borrowed capital or
loans, because if you don't have any extra capital, you're
forced to be creative from the first day. You're forced to
work long hours from the first day.

The joke is that when you start your own business, you
only have to work half-time, and you can select whichever
twelve hours of the day you prefer. You have to work a minimum of six days a week, and usually seven. The average
entrepreneur works from sixty to seventy hours a week,
which is about ten or twelve hours a day, six or seven days

a week. If you think it's possible to start a new business by working less than that, you are going to have a big surprise when you start.

I have a good friend who started a little business with posters, and he slept in his little shop for two or three years. He slept on the table and finished work in the evening, and he would sleep on the table. Then he'd get up off the table in the morning, probably eat at the corner McDonald's, and work all day. When the day was over, he'd go back to sleep on the table.

Why? Because he couldn't afford another place, and he couldn't afford to be away. He had to be working all the time.

At the beginning, everything costs much, much more than you expect—double and triple. Again: twice as much, three times as long. The amount that you can charge is largely fixed by how much customers will pay. The only way to make a greater profit is by becoming so efficient that you can produce your product or service at a lower and lower cost, and that becomes your profit.

I went through a period when I took money and put it into the business to pay my staff for two to three years. I had to actually get money from other sources. I was working at a second job in order to feed my first job, because it took that long to turn the corner, but if I hadn't done that, if I hadn't put everything back into the company, I would not have survived.

I finally did. I finally did turn the corner and did start to earn much more than it was costing me. I started to earn profits, and everything was fine.

Everybody says, "You're really lucky." That's not really the case. Many entrepreneurs have to put in everything and work twelve, sixteen hours a day for three, four, five years until they finally turn the corner and they're making more money than it's costing them to survive.

Forbes had a wonderful article some years ago. It said that every business start-up is a race against time. It's like an airplane that is diving toward the ground, crashing. The crash is when you run out of money. Can you find the formula by which you earn more than it's costing you to survive before you run out of money? It's like pulling a plane out of a dive. The business starts off. It seems like a great idea, but it immediately goes into a dive, crashing toward the ground. You are scrambling in order to bring in more money than it's costing you to survive before you run out of money. That's why intelligent investors will not invest in start-ups—because the failure rate is so high.

If I said to you, "Throw your money on the table and throw your dice; I can guarantee you a 99 percent failure rate," you'd say, "You must be kidding—a 99 percent failure rate! It's better to put the money in the bank." Better to put the money in savings, buy a mutual fund, rather than go into a 99 percent guaranteed failure rate. This is why it's so hard to raise money for a new business unless you have a track record.

Every business start-up is a race against time.
Can you find the formula by which you earn more than
it's costing you to survive before you run out of money?

If you have a track record, that's proof of concept. You have proven that you have gone through the hell of a start-up and come out the other side with a profitable business. If you've done it once, you can do it again.

I was talking to a great entrepreneur in Taiwan. I was introduced to him at a private luncheon. He was in all the business magazines. He was the Jeff Bezos of the Chinese press, and he'd come to the US. He'd gone to college in the US. He'd seen the Amazon phenomenon starting up, and he said that would be a good idea back in Taiwan.

He went back to Taiwan, and he went to visit publishers to ask them if they would sell through the online media. They all said, "No, absolutely not, because it's totally alien to the Chinese culture. Books are things that are bought personally, one-on-one, sold hand-to-hand, eye-to-eye."

He went from publisher to publisher, and there are thousands of publishers. Remember, there are 1.3 billion Chinese speakers in Asia alone. Finally he found one publisher that would sell books using his method, a modified Amazon method. He began to sell a few books, and then he began to sell more books, and then he got another publisher and another.

Chinese publishers began to realize that this was the new way of selling books. More and more of them began to make profits from book sales (and all business people really care about is making sales and making profits). So more and more began to get on board.

Now, after twelve or fifteen years, he has the Amazon of Chinese books, based in Taipei. So I said, "Geez, that was hard. It sounds like you got a lot of rejection." He said,

"If I had quit after the first 5,000 rejections, I wouldn't be here today."

"Now you have this great business," I said. "You're on the cover of the magazines, you're wealthy, drive a beautiful car, you have a chauffeur. Did you keep the whole company?"

"No," he said. "As a matter of fact, I own 3 percent of the company. I had to sell pieces of the company—1 percent, 2 percent, month after month, year after year—just to survive until the plane pulled out of the dive."

Here's another discovery. The 80/20 rule is that 80 percent of your success will come in the last 20 percent of the time that you work on your business. So you put in 80 percent of the time, and it's flat, like a long runway for an airplane. For 80 percent of the time, you don't get off the ground. You're just going full blast, 100 percent hard work, but you're not making any progress at all. Then it starts to work and you start to make a profit: you find the formula.

In the last 20 percent of the time, the plane is like a fast-flying jet; it takes off. Many people quit just before they reach that 80 percent point. They struggle, struggle, struggle, and they finally say to heck with it and walk away. It's just before the point where you'll take off, but you'll never know where that point is. That's why I said earlier that you have to decide that you will never quit.

The 80/20 Rule for Entrepreneurs:
80 percent of your success will come in the last
20 percent of the time that you work on your business.

Myth 3: If your product or service is good, you'll be successful.

When I began building businesses, it came as a shock to me that customers have limitless choices. You, the entrepreneur, like your product the way you like your child. You see this child as exceptional; every parent thinks their child is exceptional. But if you're a school principal, you have a thousand children to deal with.

When you bring your product to market, you automatically believe that it must be better. But again, customers want expediency. Customers always want to buy the fastest, cheapest, easiest—they want everything to be ER.

However, they always buy on the basis of *one* characteristic or attribute that the product has. Your product or service may have three or thirty good qualities, but customers will always look for the one quality that's most important to them. Then they will compare that quality with that of other products. The two most important words in marketing are *contrast* and *comparison*. Nobody does anything in isolation from other choices. Your product must be a superior choice to any other that will accomplish the same task.

I have a book at home called *Jobs to Be Done*. Every product or service does a job or accomplishes a task for a customer, and it must accomplish this task better than anything else that's available in the same price range. There's also what we call the *problem to be solved*. Every product or service must solve a problem for a customer. The customer wants it solved and is willing to pay for it.

I have another concept, which I call *the goal to be achieved*. Every product is aimed at achieving a goal for a customer that the customer has not yet achieved but wants to achieve. You have to show that your choice, your product's accomplishments and problem solving are superior to that of any other competitor, because if that is not the case, the customer will pass by.

Customers are heartless. They have ice water in their veins, and they only want to know what a child wants to know—what's in it for *me, me, me,* and *double me.* It must be superior to anything else that's available to *me,* or I won't buy it.

It's not "I will think about it." When a customer says to you, "Let me think about it," they're saying, "No, I will not buy it. I'm not going to think about it, because I do not see how it is superior to any other way to accomplish this goal or solve this problem." That's market fit.

A great example: Donuts are very popular, and a company came along called Krispy Kreme. Krispy Kreme had a special flavor that no other donut had. It had a particular type of caramel coating that caused the donut to taste almost illegally good. Krispy Kreme donuts went ballistic. People lined up around the block, sometimes 200 or 300 people in a row, to get these special donuts. It was in *Fortune, Forbes,* on television. Nothing had ever been seen like this: that something as common as a donut suddenly went crazy. People didn't go into the store and just buy one; they went in and bought a boxful. They didn't take them home and put them in the refrigerator; they sat on the curb outside and ate the whole boxful.

Krispy Kreme franchises were selling for a million dollars apiece. People were investing their homes, their house, their cars, their businesses in Krispy Kreme franchises. Two years later, they were broke.

What happened? Somebody wrote an article in *The New York Times* or *The Wall Street Journal*. The article showed that people who consume Krispy Kreme donuts on a regular basis put on two to three inches around their stomach almost immediately. It was the most fattening single pastry in the history of America. The market stopped. The Krispy Kreme donut franchises around the country went empty. Why? One small change. There was one reason why people went crazy over it, and one reason why nobody bought them anymore.

Myth 4: To be a successful entrepreneur, you need to invent something novel and groundbreaking.

Actually you only need to be 10 percent new or different to start a fortune. But that 10 percent has to be something that people want or need and are willing to pay for.

One way of finding a business opportunity is the *aggravation factor*. What is it that customers don't like about the way a particular product or service is sold?

One of my favorite stories is about a young guy, an orphan named Tom Monaghan, who was attending college. He had no money and no family, so he worked at delivering pizzas to the university. Students like pizzas.

Use the *Aggravation Factor* for find a business
opportunity: What is it that customers don't like about
the way a particular product or service is sold?

Each time Monaghan delivered a pizza, they would be angry with him: "Why does it take so long to get a pizza? I ordered this an hour ago?"

He would say, "The order has to be taken, the pizza has to be prepared, then it has to be baked, and boxed, and cut, and then it has to be shipped and delivered. It takes an hour, sometimes longer."

Monaghan delivered pizzas for a year, and he was observant, so he kept a note of the pizzas that people bought. He found the 80/20 rule turned out to be true: 80 percent of all the pizzas that were purchased from this pizza place—this was a mom-and-pop place—were for eight of the forty or fifty varieties that they had, and they were medium-sized.

So Monaghan went to his bosses, Luigi and Rosita, and said, "Why don't we pre-prepare these pizzas and offer them for immediate delivery? So you can say, 'If you order this pizza, you can get it within thirty or forty-five minutes.'"

They said, "No, no, no. It's not the way pizzas are pre-pared. It's not the way the pizza business works. It's not the way we've operated all of our lives." It was the comfort zone.

Monaghan still kept getting these aggravated students, because they were delivering pizzas an hour later. So he concluded that when people order a pizza, they're already hungry. They're not going to wait an hour. They want it now, and when people are hungry now, they are not very forgiving. My son calls it *hangry*. They get hangry. When they're hungry, they get angry.

So he rolled everything, like Texas hold'em. He found a bankrupt pizza restaurant two or three blocks away from where he was working, and he gave the landlord his Volkswagen—that's all he had in the world—for two months' rent. Then he borrowed some money from his friends, including his brother, who was also an orphan.

They bought the ingredients, and they pre-prepared them. He began to put up signs around the university saying, "Pizza delivered within thirty minutes, or it's free." Now that has huge appeal to students, because students don't have a lot of money. Fast, and if it's not fast, it's free.

People began to buy these pizzas. He called his company Domino's. Before the dust had settled, there were more than 8,000 Domino's Pizza restaurants around the world. Tom Monaghan, the orphan boy who started it, was worth $2.3 billion. He's one of the richest men in the world because he had one idea: when people order pizza, they're already hungry.

That's the need. That's the problem. That's the goal. People want pizza in their stomachs now. Your job is to get it to them fast.

Some people complained that Domino's Pizza was multi-plying by hundreds and thousands of stores, but the pizzas weren't as good as the ones that took sixty to ninety minutes to get. Other people said, "Who cares? It's good enough if it's fast."

Here is a penniless orphan student doing a joe job delivering pizzas in a used Volkswagen. He came up with an idea to improve just one thing: the speed at which you get the pizza. How could you increase the speed? Narrow them down, pre-prepare them, and get them out of the place ten to twelve minutes after the order comes in.

If you are an aspiring entrepreneur, your job is like a radar screen. Just continue searching the horizon for those little blips, those little things where a lot of people have a problem, an irritation or aggravation. Then ask how you could resolve that irritation. How could you solve this customer's problem? How could you make the customer happy?

Make sure there are enough customers. When I invest in any business, I always make sure that there are at least a million customers in the country who can buy this product or service. You're not going to get a million, but if you get 10,000, that's pretty good, and if you get 10,000 on a regular basis and 10,000 repeating or 10,000 renewing, then you can become very successful.

Just think about that. Think of one little thing that people are really irritated by and that they would be willing to pay to have solved for them, and then be the first person in the front of the line to solve the problem.

Myth 5: Most entrepreneurs are wild risk takers.

As I've already pointed out, successful entrepreneurs are risk avoiders in pursuit of profit. Successful entrepreneurs are those who find a way to generate profit, to provide a product or service at a cost that is less than customers are willing to pay. That's it. They do everything possible to avoid risk.

Earlier I mentioned bootstrapping. When you bootstrap, you can't make any mistakes, because you have no money. You can't afford it. If you're bootstrapping and you make a mistake, you're out of business. You lose your house, your home, your car, your bank account, and everything else, so bootstrapping forces you to be risk-averse. It forces you to think carefully about every decision in satisfying customers.

You don't speculate. You practice proof of concept. If you have a new idea, you try it out on a small scale so that if it does not work, if it fails for any reason at all, your loss is very small, and you can cut it quickly.

There was an interesting book written a few years ago called *The Zurich Axioms*. It's to help people become wealthy. What are the secrets of the people in Zurich who supposedly control half the money in the world?

Number one is, they cut their losses. They proceed very carefully, and as soon as they feel that they made a mistake, they cut their losses quickly. So cut your losses.

I have a good friend who plays professional Texas hold'em poker. He's a very smart guy. He told me something that I thought was really neat. He said that every time you make a bet or take a card, look at the table as though it's a brand-new table. Forget about how much you've bet already. Forget about how many cards you've taken. That's the past. You cannot change the past. You

---

The #1 Insight of *The Zurich Axioms*: As soon as you feel
you have made a mistake, cut your losses quickly.

---

look at the table anew, and you make your next decision
based on the way the table is *now*. If the table is not good
now, if the cards have changed, if it's clear that someone
else probably has a better hand than you, cut your losses.
Get out immediately.

It's astonishing how many people think that if they
throw good money after bad, somehow the bad money
will become good. They're offering a product or service
that nobody wants, so they double their advertising
budget—and people who sell advertising will tell you all
day long that all you need to do is spend more money
advertising. Your bum product, which nobody wants,
will suddenly become like Cinderella, and people will
start to buy it. No.

I have a friend who owns a restaurant, very successful, very wealthy. He started as an immigrant from Italy,
with nothing going for him. He worked in a restaurant
as a dishwasher and then as a waiter. I met him shortly
after he came from Italy. I was talking to him and asking him questions, and I said, "Geez, this guy has real
quality." Just the way he waited on tables, the way he
served you—everything. This guy was taking his craft
very seriously.

Eventually the guy bought a cheap restaurant. Every
single evening, all evening long, he checked the garbage
cans at the back to see what people were throwing away.

If they threw something away, he would go back to the table and say, "Thank you very much for coming to my restaurant. I get the impression that you don't like this particular dish. Could you tell me why?" People said, "Sure." People are very open to venting their frustration. They bought the food, and they've thrown it away.

If people didn't like the dish, he would cut it out. He would keep cutting the dishes. His goal was to make sure there was no thrown-away food in the trash can. By the time he was finished after two or three years, he had four restaurants and was a multimillionaire, one of the most respected people in the city, and written up in the newspapers. People waved to him when he walked down the streets.

But his idea was, cut your losses quickly. If customers tell you that they don't like it by not buying it or chucking it away, discontinue it immediately. Don't keep thinking, "I'll just put out bigger portions of this food that nobody wants," which is the equivalent of spending more money advertising or dressing up the packaging.

Myth 6: Most entrepreneurs are financially successful.

I've developed a very simple formula that I've used all over the world for thousands of businesses. I ask, "Why are some businesses more successful than others?"

I joke with my audiences. I say, "I have done a survey among your customers before offering this seminar today, and I found a most remarkable thing. All of your customers have one desire in common. They all want you to be rich. I couldn't believe it. They all want you to be rich. They think about making you rich all the time."

Of course, people are blank-faced when they hear this, and they go, "What?" I say, "Yes, they want you to make them happy, and if they're happy with a product or service that they're using now, they want you to make them happier than your competitor is making them. They want you to make them happy, and they want you to sell lots of stuff to them and make lots of money so that you can become rich."

How do you find out what your customers want in order to be happy? Go and ask them. They will tell you. I've worked with some of the biggest and best companies in the world, and I've done all kinds of studies on the way that they plan, design, and strategize. They have a special obsession with asking their customers, "Thank you, thank you, thank you for buying from us. How can we make you happier next time? What can we do more of or less of? What can we start doing or stop doing? Please tell us, because we want you to be happy."

This has a very positive effect on customers. Customers will tell you, willingly and in detail. Sometimes a customer will give you just one idea to make him or her happy personally, and it will proliferate like a chain reaction throughout all your customer base and cause your sales and your profitability to go through the roof.

Most companies, 80 percent, are in the bottom 80 percent. (Oh my, what an incredible revelation!) They struggle all their lives. If you want to be in the top 20 percent, you find out what companies in the top 20 percent offer to their customers that is different. What is it? Then do it.

I was guilty of this for many years. It's astonishing when people say, "Yes, I know that would makes my customers happier, but I don't want to do it. It moves me out of my comfort zone. It causes me to do something different than I'm used to doing."

If you want to play with the big boys, treat your customers the way the big boys do. You make the customers happier and happier, and you keep asking them how you can make them happy.

One company I work with that I greatly admire is Hewlett-Packard. Hewlett-Packard started off in a garage. It's now an icon in Silicon Valley. Hewlett and Packard started from the very beginning by asking every single customer in multiple ways, "Are you happy? How did you like the product? Is the product good? Are you going to buy it again? How can we improve it?"

They would phone them. They would visit them personally. They would write to them. They would send them surveys. They were constantly asking them, "How can we make you happier next time?"

Don't make the mistake of asking, "How was everything?" because the answer is, "Everything was fine, but I won't be back." They don't say the second part, but

---

Find out what companies in the Top 20 percent offer
to their customers that is different. Then do it—
even if it moves you out of your comfort zone.

---

when a customer has no complaints or says, "Everything is fine, I have no complaints," according to follow-up research, the customer is on their way out the door and is not coming back, and none of their friends are coming back either.

Never ask a person, "How was it last time?" Say, "How can we make you happier next time?" Those are the magic words, based on $22 million of research. If you want to increase the size of your business and become successful, always ask, "How can we do it better next time?"

Myth 7: Entrepreneurs are born, not made.

Entrepreneurship is a natural and spontaneous expression of the human personality. People are natural entrepreneurs from the time they're children. When my children were small, they would sit along the edge of the golf course, and when golf balls were knocked off into the brush, they would go and get them. They would sit there until the golfers came along. They'd say, "I found your ball in the brush. I'll give it back to you for fifty cents." People would say, "Sure. It's certainly much easier than going looking for it myself. It's a three-dollar golf ball." Then my wife would sell Coca-Cola bottles that she picked up along the street or along the highway. She'd sell soft-drink bottles and make two cents from a soft-drink bottle.

People are natural entrepreneurs because of the normal human drive for survival and for "thrival." Human beings are also opportunistic. They look for ways to improve their condition. They look for expediency, so the entrepreneurial nature in human beings actually flips the 80/20 rule around. Probably 80 percent of people have entrepreneurial instincts. Maybe 20 percent don't, for a variety of reasons that we can't predict.

Anybody can be an entrepreneur. The essence of entrepreneurship is to look for a way to create value for yourself by creating value for others. What can I do to create value for other people and then keep a little? If you're really good at it, you do it again, and you do it again.

You set up one McDonald's restaurant, which is very successful at selling hamburgers and French fries and malts very quickly and fresh, and now you have 36,000 of them. Why? Every single one of them is focused on making the customer happy, and making them happier than the other fast-food restaurant somewhere else.

Everybody has the ability to be entrepreneurial, just as everybody has the ability to ride a bicycle or drive a car or even fly an airplane, but this doesn't mean that you can do it automatically. You have the ability, but you have to develop it, just as everybody has the ability to play certain sports, at least to an average level or above-average level, but you have to work at it, and you have to practice.

That's what I learned: if you can study entrepreneurship and sales and marketing, understand customers, and ask questions and listen, you can get better and better at making people happy for less and less time and money, and the difference is your profit.

Myth 8: All entrepreneurs want to be rich.

Everyone wants to be financially well-off. Everyone wants to be financially independent. Everybody wants to go to a restaurant and order off the menu without looking at the right-hand column to see how much the dish costs. That's just normal and natural, but it's not why people start businesses.

When people start businesses, often they have stars in their eyes. They think they'll make a lot of money, but they want more than anything else to be free. It's to *not* be under the control of someone else, to *not* have someone else telling them what to do, especially if they're working for a boss who is not pleasant or polite or supportive. They hate the idea of having to put up with this boss just because they have to pay their bills.

The ideal of being free is so powerful because human beings, above all other things, love freedom, especially financial freedom. I just read my friend Wayne Dyer's observations about success. He said success is the ability to live your life your own way, doing what you want to do, with people that you want to do it with, without being concerned about the price of things.

In other words, happiness is to be free. That's the major drive and motivation. Only a small number of entrepre-

---

"Success is the ability to live your life your own way, doing what you want to do, with people that you want to do it with, without being concerned about the price of things."
—Wayne Dyer

---

neurs will become wealthy, but these are people who are very clear that they want to become wealthy.

One thing I've been teaching the last few years is that nobody becomes wealthy accidentally. You have to make a decision that you are, in the course of your career, going to make a lot of money. If you're going to make a lot of money, you have to ask that magic question: how? Then you look at other people who started with nothing and are successful and ask how they did it. If you're not sure, go and ask them.

I have a friend who came over from England many years ago. He got a job selling advertising space for a specialty magazine, a yacht magazine or a boat magazine. He sold lots of space. One day he called on a prospective customer, a person who owned a business, and offered to sell him advertising space. This fellow declined. He didn't buy it from him, but he liked him, so he gave some advice. He said, "Have you ever thought of doing this or offering that or offering this?"

My friend developed a habit of meeting with this man—this older man, very successful, very wealthy—for lunch. He met him for lunch once a month and took notes. Today my friend owns thirty-one magazines. Every magazine has made a profit every single month for more than thirty years, which is unheard of in that world. It was because he got advice from this older and wiser man.

He wrote a book. I think his friend's name is Ray. It was called *Lunch with Ray*. He sent me a copy of it. He's very smart, respected by everybody, a fine man, rich beyond belief. He would just ask Ray for advice, and once a month he would meet him for lunch at a beautiful restaurant and listen while he gave him advice on how to be successful in business if he was having problems.

When I spoke to him, my friend had 300 managers running his magazines, with all the publicists and advertising people and writers and editors. He'd started off in the magazine business as one person knocking on doors, selling space, getting advice from other people.

It's really important to keep asking for advice with a long-term goal of being successful. My friend had a fantasy that one day he would own a magazine, and he'd be able to do everything except write the articles. He'd be able to sell the advertising and do the financing and everything else.

He began to study magazine publishing. He had no knowledge about it at first, but today he's extremely wealthy. He attributes it all to asking people like Ray for advice on how to be more successful in this field.

My friend said that after thirty-one years, Ray never bought a single bit of advertising from him. But he did give him advice, and that was one reason Ray became wealthy.

Myth 9: Entrepreneurs have no personal lives.

Every year I go to a resort in Hawaii with my family. We started going thirty years ago. At that time, we stayed in a very small unit, with our family jammed in. As time passed, we stayed at larger and larger places, and now we stay at a very large place.

We have gotten an opportunity to meet other people who come to this resort, and they are 80/20: 80 percent are entrepreneurs, people who started with nothing and worked their way up. One regular guest is one of the richest men in the world, and he has bought three or four huge units facing the ocean. He brings in his whole family and his family's families.

If you ask these people, "What's the most important thing in life to you?" they always say it's their family. They care about their family more than anything else. If they have to make a choice between anything—the business, money, anything—family comes first. Family games, family recitals, family graduations, family anything. It's always their family.

Becoming wealthy doesn't make you wring your hands with lots of money like Scrooge McDuck. It just gives you the opportunity to take better care of your family and to provide a wonderful life for them. If you look back on your life at any time, you'll find it was the things that you did with your family, the people you love and the people who love you, that are more important than anything else.

Entrepreneurs, mainly male but also many females, will work sixty hours a week to provide for their family. It's to make sure that their family is OK, that they can do the things that they want to do. They can be free. I know, because this is my motivation: to organize my life so that my family has choices. They can do whatever they want to do.

Entrepreneurs are motivated at the beginning, as everybody is, with the desire to become financially independent, to have enough money that they don't worry about money or stay awake at night. As soon as they reach that point of surviving and thriving, money becomes a secondary concern to them.

Money is like a scorecard in sports. It's very important to track it on a regular basis so you can tell how well you're doing. Are you using your time well? Are you using it better doing this rather than doing that? But it's only a scorecard.

If you talk to self-made millionaires and multimillionaires, more than anything else they talk about their kids, their families. The other things they talk about is how hard they had to work coming up and the big mistakes they made and how much money they lost. Every one of them made big mistakes and lost a lot of money, but you never hear them talk about their money. They never talk about their success or about their houses or cars or boats.

Their major concern is always talking about the people in their lives. So being a successful entrepreneur gives you a wonderful freedom to do whatever you want to do with the most important people in your world.

Money is like a scorecard in sports. It's very important to track it on a regular basis so you can tell how well you're doing.

3

Essential #1
What Type of Business Should I Start?

The first essential to start and succeed in your own business, is the foundation, the root system from where your success will emerge: What type of business should you start?

It really comes down to emotion. It comes down to heart. It comes down—not to passion; *passion* is an overworked word—but to something that attracts you.

Many years ago I was flying in first class back to San Diego. I was talking to a woman about where we lived. She lived in a very nice neighborhood, better than mine (although I lived in a good neighborhood).

She asked, "How did you choose your house?"

I said, "We looked at 150 houses and finally decided on this one."

"It grabbed you, honey, didn't it?" she said.

It grabbed you: I never forgot that. There was something that reached out and clutched at you.

Successful entrepreneurs are producing and selling and making available something that *grabbed them*. They love it. It appeals to their heart, and there are many different dimensions here. First of all, they love the product, and they especially love the product for themselves.

Inc. magazine is probably the best magazine for small and medium-sized enterprises. They do all kinds of surveys, and they keep a running record of the 500 fastest-growing companies in the United States.

When they began producing this study, I was amazed, because the fastest-growing company that year grew 14,800 times in 3 years. Last year, the fastest-growing company grew 16,900 times in 3 years. Arguably, these companies started off small, but imagine growing 10,000 or 15,000 times.

The average company in the Inc. 500 grew 17 times in 3 years. I ask my clients in my seminars, "What difference would it make in your life if your business grew 17 times in 3 years—17 times the number of staff, 17 times the number of buildings, 17 times the number of products and services being delivered? Imagine 100 times or 1,000 times." These business owners are shocked at this number. I say, "Hundreds of companies are doing this every year, and it's because they find something that appeals to a lot of people at the right time."

Reporters interviewed the founders of these Inc. 500 companies and asked them, "How did you get into that particular business?" and 95 percent of them—almost a clean sweep—said they found this product or service that they really liked. They liked it so much that they wanted it for themselves and for their families. When they began to produce it, buy it, import it, or manufacture it for their families, their neighbors and friends said, "That's really neat. Can I get that?"

One of my favorite stories is about an immigrant couple who came from Europe, I think it was Turkey, and they had two little children in school. They were good citizens, they attended PTA meetings, and they were really concerned about their kids doing well. The kids were less than ten years old. The parents found that you could create lessons on an iPad that their kids could use to do their homework lessons. They also found that the school could make the lessons available on the iPad, and their kids loved to watch television. So the parents tinkered around at home and came up with this program whereby the kids would have to do a certain amount of homework, and then they could watch a certain amount of kids' TV. Then it would click off. Then the kids would do a certain amount of homework, and again they could watch a certain amount of kids' TV. The parents introduced it to their children, and they loved it.

Reporters have found that 95 percent of the founders of Inc. 500 companies said they got into their particular business by finding a product or service that they really liked.

It was like a horse and carrot. The kids came home eagerly. They couldn't watch television until they'd done a lesson. After they did a lesson, then they could watch a little television. The kids started to look forward to coming home and doing lessons.

Within four or five months, they were the top A students in the school, and they received awards at the PTA meetings. Parents came up and said, "Geez, how did your kids get such good grades?" They said, "We devised this little system to incentivize our kids to do their homework. We spoke to the teachers, and the teachers have cooperated with us. They were very helpful. They thought it was a neat idea, so the teachers began to help them with the lessons, and we put it all together."

"Can we have that for our kids?"

"Sure," they said, and gave it to them.

The other parents said, "No, no. You can't just give it away. You have to charge something."

So they charged something. It went viral, and it grew 14,800 times in three years. They became one of the fastest-growing companies, became wealthy beyond belief.

They started because they wanted this product for themselves and their own families, so that's a really good measure: Do you want the product for yourself and your family? Do you like the product so much that you want your family to have access to it? That's the starting point. Then sometimes it becomes a business.

One famous story is about the man who started eBay. His name is Pierre Omidyar, and he had collected Pez dispensers for years and years. People who collect Pez dispensers are like stamp collectors. They like to sell and trade them to other people. He thought, "How could we do this?" and he developed a little system which became eBay. People could trade Pez dispensers on it.

People said, "What else could you trade?" It became eBay, and he's now a billionaire, one of the richest men in the world, but he started this for himself and for his friends so that they could trade their Pez dispensers. He developed a little program so that you could put the picture and details on it. It was something you and I would never even think of. Everybody else would get onto it, and they began to trade more and more and more things.

So the first question you have to ask is, how do you feel about the product? On the way to becoming successful as an entrepreneur, you're going to have many obstacles and setbacks and difficulties, and you're going to have losses and failures and frustrations. You're going to lose heart. But if you love the product and see how good it can be for you and for others, you will never give up. You will find a way to make it work.

Successful entrepreneurs start off by loving the product. The second thing is they love their customers, and this is really important. If you can imagine a barbell with love on one end and love on the other end and the bar in between, it's like that.

Success starts off with *what?* What is the product, and what is the value offering, and what difference does this product make in the lives of others that's really important to them? When you hear that someone has used the product and improved their life in some way, it makes you happy. You don't get happy because they paid you money for it. You get happy because they tell you success stories of what happened with the product.

In regard to multilevel marketing (MLM): people get into MLM companies because they're promised to make a lot of money. However, if you talk to MLM people—and I have spoken to probably a million of them in eighty countries—and if you ask them why they got into this business, it's that the MLM company had usually one product that was really good. They experienced the goodness and the benefit of that product, and they wanted other people to experience the same thing.

One company developed a vitamin formulation. It was fastidiously developed. It was based on a formulation going back seventy-five or eighty years, and it was tested at seventeen universities; it's constantly being tested and upgraded. It dramatically reduced the incidence of colds and flus. If you had any kind of ailment, including surgery, the recovery time was 50 percent or less than what it would usually be. If you took it, you had better hair, better skin, better everything. You will notice a difference the day you take it. You will have more energy, you will sleep better at night, you will wake more refreshed, and so on. People say, "That sounds pretty good," so they try it out, often on a free sample basis, and they actually feel the physical difference. They make sure that all their family members are taking it.

Other products are available through MLM—nutritional products, beauty products, cleansing products. Every one of them has a story, and every one of them (the successful ones anyway) has been exhaustively developed so that it's really good. If you use it, you notice the difference.

When one of these MLM people says, "Let me tell you about this business opportunity," they don't tell you how you can make all this money. They explain to you how if you like it and you buy it, you can buy it at a discount. If you sell it to other people, you can sell it to them at a discount and earn part of it back so that you'll benefit, your customer will benefit, and the person who invited you to the business will benefit. This is how MLM works worldwide.

However, there are hundreds of MLM businesses that come and go over the years. Why is that? I've watched them very carefully, and the answer is, the product doesn't work. It has a lot of hype. You can make a lot of money by getting a lot of other people into this, but it doesn't work. People don't go into the business with the proper motivation. The motivation is to get rich, and getting rich is never enough of a motivation to keep you going when you experience the inevitable adversities of business life. You have to love the product. You have to care about it.

You also have to care about the people you sell it to. People who are successful in business don't talk about how much they're selling or how much money they're making. They talk about customer stories. That's all they talk about. They get together, and I'm not just talking about MLM now. I'm talking about every kind of product or service that's really successful.

When the people in those companies get together, they talk about happy customers. They talk about this person and that person who was able to do this and was able to achieve that and able to change this and so on. They bring their happy customers to company celebrations, and the customers get up and say, "I used this product, and this is the difference it made in my life."

So you have to love the product, and the product has to be *efficacious*. The product has to work. Does the advertising work? Does the product work? Does the distribution method work? Does the sales process work? The most important question in all of business is, does it work?

The second part is the customers. Who are the customers, and where are they? What do they want and need more than anything else? How can we help them improve their lives and work?

Human beings are designed so that the greatest joy they get in life is helping other people, serving other people, doing something that enhances the life or work of other people. That's what makes people shine and makes them happy.

If you're selling something that you really like, ask this question: Would you sell this product to your mother? Would you sell this product to your father or your brother or your sister or your best friend or your aunt or uncle? Would you eagerly explain this product to third parties, to strangers? It's one-on-one selling. You look in the eyeball of the other person and tell them, "This is good for you." They use it, and they're persuaded.

I was in the lobby of a hotel in Houston, and I was checking out. There was a meeting, and everyone was laughing and talking. I asked one of the people, "What's going on in there?"

Human beings are designed so that the greatest joy they get in life is helping other people, serving other people, doing something that enhances the life or work of other people.

"It's a business meeting," he said.

"What kind of a business is it?"

He explained that it was for a certain product. I said, "Wow, that's interesting. I like that idea. I could sell it. I'm traveling. I'm leaving Houston and going back to Vancouver, British Columbia."

"Let me give you some information," he said, "and if you'd like to try it out, I'll fix you up." That was it. In the lobby of a hotel, and I've been using the product ever since 1972.

Why? He was happy, and they were all happy. They were all enthusiastic and warm and charming and just wanted people to experience the product.

Then you have to ask yourself whom you are selling to. In marketing, we always say, the most important word is the question the owl asks in the high woods: *Who? Who? Who?*

Next, you have to think about the method of selling the product or service. Is it in harmony with your personality? You wouldn't want to stand on street corners selling something, because you wouldn't be comfortable doing that. The product could be a good product, and the customer could be a nice person, but you're not going to sell on the street corner. So the methods of sales and delivery, and customer service, all have to fit.

If you and I were to go to a buffet, we would walk along the buffet; you would have your plate, and I would have mine. When we got back to the table, your plate would be totally different from mine. It's the same with human beings. What each person requires to be happy and satisfied is completely different from what someone else requires.

So it has to make you happy, and this is really the most important thing. You'll find that people who work for the big companies, the booming companies, the companies that are legends like Google and Apple and Microsoft, and so on—these people are happy. You go to those companies, and everybody's happy. They laugh, they help each other. If they don't, if they don't laugh and they're not happy, they get them out of there really fast. The fastest way that you can lose a job at one of these great companies is not to be happy at your work.

People look forward to going to work. I've told you a little bit about Hewlett-Packard. Hewlett-Packard created a work environment such that people loved to go to work. They loved to go to work so much that they went to work early, and they stayed later. Then they would start to go to work on Saturday and Sunday.

The company said, "This is not a good idea. You should be spending time with your family on the weekends."

But the employees loved to go to work. The company had to lock the doors and put security guards on the main building in Palo Alto so employees couldn't get in on the weekends. Even so, they found ways to get around the guards and unlock the doors from the inside, or they would have a spy inside who would unlock the door.

It became almost like a police game, where the security people were trying to catch the employees who wanted to go to work.

They loved the products, they loved the services, they loved the customers, and they loved what they were doing. That's the highest level. If you go to the Inc. 500, the fastest-growing companies probably in the world, it's the same thing. They love the work.

So the first question you ask is, do you love the product or service? Does it grab you? If you don't know very much about it and you're not very experienced, then you can't sell it very well.

At the beginning, you may not love it. You may be neutral about it, or skeptical. Most people are a little bit skeptical. Sometimes you need to learn more about the product or service, which is why a good company, on day one, will teach you about the product and how it works to help people. They immerse you, sometimes for a week or two weeks. They put you through product orientation so that you understand what the product does. When you do, you go, "Wow! This is really neat." You start to love the product because it makes a difference in the lives of other people. It makes other people happy.

I'll give you another example. At one point Walt Disney, who was directing movies in Hollywood, and his brother Roy were visiting Tivoli Gardens, which is like the Central Park of Copenhagen. It's considered to be the most beautiful amusement park in the world. It has lakes and trees and flowers and music and bands playing and families walking around. Many people go to Europe to go to Copenhagen to go to the Tivoli Gardens.

So they were sitting there in the Tivoli Gardens, and Walt said something that would change the history of the world: "Do you notice anything about this park?" Roy looked around: lots of people; people were happy.

"There's not a speck on the ground," said Walt. "There's not a matchstick," and that was at a time when a lot of people smoked. "There's not a candy wrapper, there's nothing. You could eat off the ground. In the United States, you walk through amusement parks and your feet are covered with gum and guck. Here it's impeccably clean. What if we were to build something like that in the United States? Families would bring their kids, because families don't want their kids walking around in dirt." That was the beginning of Disneyland.

If you go through Disneyland, you will not see a speck on the ground. Senior executives, the senior mucky-mucks, will be walking along, and if somebody drops a French fry or a piece of paper, they will swoop in like a raven and pick it up. It will not even hit the ground. That's what they teach people: these are our guests, and this is their home for the day, just as you would want your guests to be in a clean environment and be happy and healthy.

Their motto for Disneyland is D.R.E.A.M—dream: Disney Resort Experiences Are Magic. Everybody who works in Disneyland—they call them cast members—wants to make this a magic experience for those people. The stories about the way they do this are phenomenal.

They only hire people who love the idea of creating an environment where everybody's happy. If you go to Disneyland, the one sound that you hear all the time is laughter. People are laughing all the time. Everywhere you go, people are laughing. The Disney resort experiences are magic.

We have a hospital chain here in San Diego called Scripps. Scripps has been rated as one of the top ten hospital chains in the world. I've been to Scripps. I've had surgery and medical treatments there, and so has my family. Two of my children were born there.

I studied Scripps a little, and I found that some years ago, they replaced their president with a man who worked for an insurance company. They put him in charge of this hospital, which is now a hospital chain. He conducted a study with the Peter F. Drucker Foundation for Nonprofit Management. They asked, "What is the purpose of a hospital?" The answer had been the same for hundreds of years. It's to bring health and wellness to sick and injured people. OK. The consultants said, "No, that's not true. By the time a person comes to the hospital, they're already sick. They're already injured. They're already unwell. The hospital can do nothing to stop or to prevent that."

"So now the person comes to the hospital. What's the purpose of the hospital? Their primary concern is nervousness, attention, fear. What's going to happen? What's going to happen to my family member? The goal of the hospital is to give reassurance. *This* is the purpose. It's to give reassurance, so that when people come there, they are reassured that they're OK. Their family member is OK. Everything is fine."

The analysts then asked what other institutions have this same philosophy. First-class hotels. The Four Seasons, Hyatt Regency, and so on. So they said, "We're going to run this hospital like an excellent hotel. We're going to take care of our guests as if they were coming to a first-class hotel."

At Scripps hospitals, they treat you and your family members with kindness, with courtesy, with warmth, with friendliness. They take you where you want to go. They smile. They're friendly. They're quick. They treat you as if you were in a first-class hotel, and they've become one of the most successful hospital chains in the world because of this philosophy.

It's the same thing with building a successful business. How are you going to treat your customers? How are you going to treat people who use your service? You're going to treat them like guests at a first-class hotel.

Companies like this only hire people who care about the people they serve. There was a famous advertising line some years ago. It said, "We don't hire people and teach them to be nice. We only hire nice people."

Southwest Airlines is the most profitable airline in the world and has been every single month, every single year, practically forever. Its whole focus is to make customers feel happy and cared for and to have them feel they made the right choice.

Southwest is a low-cost airline. They have single-type planes—no first class. They don't serve any meals, yet

> When building a successful business, plan to treat
> your customers like guests at a first-class hotel.

they're the most profitable darn airline in the world, and they're full all the time. You take it, and why? It's because they have this general approach of making people feel really good and treating you well.

There's a restaurant chain—no names need be mentioned. It's very fast-growing because they're really great cost-cutters. They bought another chain that had 600 restaurants. The day they took over, they cut the size of the buns and loaves of bread by 60 or 70 percent. The quality of the food dropped. The quality of the service dropped.

I'd been going to this restaurant for twenty years. I went three times in the following month or two, and the drop in quality was consistent every time. Two different restaurants, the same thing.

It turned out that this company has one goal in life. It's to screw the diners by giving them smaller portions and worse food. This is a steak restaurant. The steak was inedible, and I spoke to the maître d's whom I'd known for years, who said, "It's the new boss, the new owners. There's nothing that we can do."

The maître d's had worn tuxedos. Now they were forced to wear plain suits. Everything went downhill. My wife and I used to go to that restaurant twice a month. We haven't been there twice in a year. We don't go anymore, and nobody else goes anymore.

These people care more about the additional profit on a small loaf of bread than they do about making their customers happy. They had the idea that the customers who can afford to go to an expensive restaurant don't know the difference in the quality of the food. The staff are equally nice, but the new owners have basically killed this restaurant chain. Why? It was taken over by people who didn't love their customers.

Up until that time, you'd walk into that restaurant, they were happy to see you and smiling and charming, and they'd take you to your table. They'd call you by name. It was a real experience: you'd look forward to going out for dinner—until the new management took over.

This happens over and over again. A company is successful, and financers buy it, and they come in. They say, "We can really loot this company. We have all this business. People are paying premium prices, so we're going to raise the prices and lower the quality."

When that happens, the answer is, you walk. You just walk.

Never compromise your integrity. Your integrity is the quality with which you do your work, the quality with which you provide your product or service, the quality with which you treat your customers. This is who you are.

So when we talk about the best kind of job, company, product, service for you, it's always one that grabs you. You can hardly wait to go to work. You love to go to work. You love to go to work and see your coworkers. You love to see your customers. You feel happy doing it. That releases something inside of you that makes you a much better

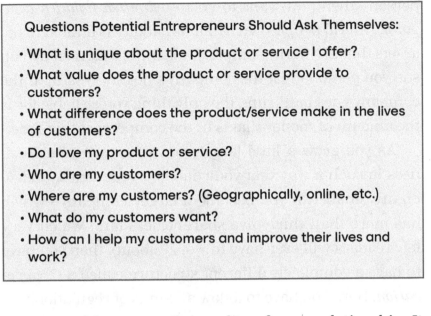

Questions Potential Entrepreneurs Should Ask Themselves:

- What is unique about the product or service I offer?
- What value does the product or service provide to customers?
- What difference does the product/service make in the lives of customers?
- Do I love my product or service?
- Who are my customers?
- Where are my customers? (Geographically, online, etc.)
- What do my customers want?
- How can I help my customers and improve their lives and work?

person and increases the quality of your relationship. It makes you happy.

Everything that's good in your work as an entrepreneur comes when you really care about your product and your customers.

Let's turn now to the types of businesses you can start. The ones I want to discuss here are the following: a sole proprietorship or home-based business, a limited-liability corporation, an S-corporation, and a franchise.

The simplest of all is a *sole proprietorship*. A sole proprietorship is where you buy a product at a certain price, you sell it to someone, a customer, at a higher price, and you make a profit. The profit is what is reported for accounting and taxation purposes.

If your company starts to grow larger so that there is more than one person—*sole*, after all, means only one person—then you want to go to a *limited-liability company*: several people own it, but its liability is limited to the assets that are in the company, meaning that nobody can sue you personally if the company's not successful. If the company goes bankrupt, the only thing you're liable for is the amount of money that is in the company at this time.

As you grow a little larger, you structure your business in such a way that your liability, your taxes, and so on are smaller. If you become a larger company—which has more than thirty-five shareholders (and which very few readers will ever have to worry about), then you have to have a completely different structure called a *C corporation*. Here you have to follow all kinds of regulations.

In every case, you always ask a lawyer. By the way, one thing I learned at great cost to me is that you never try to save money on professional advice when you're starting a business.

People say, "Why do these lawyers charge you all this money?" A lawyer has usually spent many years developing experience and knowledge about the best way to structure a business in the interest of the shareholders. If you're a small company, the amount of advice that you need is very small, and the amount that they will charge you is small as well. If you are going to start a business of any kind other than a sole proprietorship, then you ask a lawyer.

You're not going to the New York law firms. You ask a friend who has a lawyer who has an office around the corner. You say, "This is my business." You write it all down and ask, "Could you tell me the best way to structure the business at this time?" They'll take a look at it, and often they'll tell you over the phone. They'll maybe charge you $100.

Earlier in my career, I had a good lawyer, and my business was thriving. I avoided asking him for advice because he cost $500 an hour. Once I got a contract from someone for a part of my business activities. I looked at it, and I decided, "I can make this decision. It's pretty straightforward." So I signed the contract.

There were changes in the tax law, in the corporate structure, and in the standard contract. I missed something that cost me thousands of dollars, because the people who present you with contracts to sign are not your friends.

I spoke to my lawyer about this. I said, "I didn't want to spend the $500." He said, "Brian, not spending money on legal fees is the worst loss of money that you can have. You can sometimes make one mistake that a lawyer will pick up in a few seconds."

They actually know exactly where to look and can save you hours. My contract took hours to sort it out, with all kinds of conflict and threatened lawsuits. Don't do that. Pay the little extra money to get professional advice.

With regard to accountants: accounting law, especially the tax law, is so complicated today that nobody can possibly figure it out. So get a good medium-sized accountant that deals with small and medium-sized companies, and ask them for their advice.

Once I started a business, and I had some problems with an employee. I was going to fire her, because she was bad. She was stealing, and I had evidence. I asked my accountant. I said, "What do you think about this?"

"Stop. Stop. Time out," he said. "Do not do anything to mess with the labor law. This is California, where the labor laws are designed to encourage people to engage in behaviors that cause you to fire them so they can sue you. The average settlement for firing a person arbitrarily is about $74,000. Even though the person was basically witnessed, signed, sealed, and almost photographed stealing, if you fire them, it's going to cost you $74,000 and take nine months in court."

"What do you suggest I do?"

"Get a labor lawyer. A labor lawyer is going to cost a lot of money. They're going to save you more money."

A good accountant, a good lawyer will save you $5 for every $1 that you pay them. Sometimes $10, sometimes $100; sometimes a fortune. Sometimes they'll save your business. Never go cheap on professional services.

Some people use online services like LegalZoom. If it's just yourself as an entrepreneur, LegalZoom is designed for you. I've used LegalZoom for simple documents, and I've never had a problem. They have a vested interest in making sure that their services are good. They help you do very simple things, and they send you a fill-in-the-blanks contract. You simply fill in the blanks, the names, the numbers, the people, the percentages, and so on. That's all you really need. It's only when it gets complicated and you have more than one person involved and more than one liability and so on. Then you ask a lawyer for advice.

A good accountant, a good lawyer will save you
$5 for every $1 you pay them.

The legal profession hates LegalZoom, because they will charge you a tenth of what a lawyer will charge and give you exactly the same thing. Like LegalZoom, most lawyers use standard documents. They just put in a couple of names and numbers, but they charge you as if they had developed this document exclusively for you, with the number of hours that would have been involved.

Let's turn to *franchises*. Franchises have been studied to death. Anything in the world that is known about franchises is available online. You can let your fingers do the walking. You can get all the research that you need.

I studied this at great length, because I started a franchise. I own a franchise with 150 members in 22 countries, so I'm not unfamiliar with the subject. One thing I learned is that a franchise is a proven money-making system.

In other words, McDonald's started the business, and they developed the systems to make the business work. Then they sell the system to a new person, and they train the person in the system. You have to go through two or three or six months at McDonald's International Institute of Hamburgerology to get your operating license. Then they will keep in touch with you, supervise you, and make sure that you are following the system.

It's very much like a recipe. In a restaurant franchise, they teach you to cook with this recipe. They train you, they supervise you, they check on you, and they make darn sure you do not deviate from the recipe, because the recipe is what causes people to buy and buy again. It's a proven success system, and you follow the system. Whether you're paying $50,000 or $500,000 for a franchise, you're buying a proven system.

Recently I was talking to a friend of mine, a sales trainer who wanted to start his own business, and he did. He bought a franchise, a system on how to sell sales training. He paid many thousands of dollars, plus royalties, to get the right to offer that system through himself. He is a one-person franchise. I hadn't heard of that before, but you'll find that almost everything is franchised. The critical thing is, does it work? Remember, does it work, does it work, does it work?

The person selling the franchise has a vested interest in your buying it, so they will say, "Yes, it works." Franchise law says that the company must make available all the names, addresses, phone numbers, backgrounds, and financial experience of all franchises worldwide, so that you can check and double-check on those people. The company must provide you with all the statistics: how long they've been in business, how fast they've grown, how much money they have made, how profitable they are, how profitable the franchises are, and so on. So if you're going to buy a franchise, do your homework. Due diligence. Never forget those words *due diligence*.

It's astonishing how many—all the best companies in America, maybe the best companies in the world—study a business investment to death before they make a decision. They will announce that they're going to buy a particular company or go into a particular type of business, and they'll also announce a six-month due diligence period in which they will investigate every single claim that you made.

Let's go on to multilevel marketing systems: MLMs. You can start an MLM for as little as $25, so you can start with a multilevel marketing company even if you're starting with nothing. Everything is done. All you have to do is follow the system.

Now here's an important point: all business is based on selling. I often ask my audiences, "Why do you get up in the morning and go to work?" There's a silence as they mutter. I say, "The answer is to make more money. That's why you go to work, to make more money. You don't get up in the morning and go to work to make less money or to make the same amount. You want to make *more* money. Is that true?" Everybody agrees. I say, "Now how do you make more money? I call this MMM. The reason you work is MMM. So how do you MMM? The answer is SMS, which is sell more stuff."

You MMM by SMSing. So from the time you get up for the rest of the day, when are you actually working? The only time you're working is when you're selling more stuff. Never forget, and never take your eye off the ball.

"Now, how do you *make more money*?
I call this MMM. . . . The answer is SMS,
which is *sell more stuff.*"
—Brian Tracy

> **Types of businesses you can start**
>
> 1. Sole Proprietorship
> 2. LLC—Limited Liability Company
> 3. C Corporation
> 4. Franchises
> 5. MLM—Multi-Level Marketing Company

The best, biggest international companies hammer on sales every day. They measure sales every week. They measure sales every month. Everybody's promoted on the basis of their sales and the sales of people below them.

Never take your eye off the ball. It's like driving a high-powered car down a winding mountain road in the middle of a rainstorm. Never take your eye off the road, and the eye is on sales. It's selling more stuff.

The only time you're working is when you're selling more stuff. If you're not selling stuff, if you're talking to your friends, if you're checking your email, reading the newspaper, and so on, then you might as well go back home to bed, pull the covers up over your head, and go back to sleep, because you're of no use to yourself or anyone else.

Once the best structure is put in place, it's like the foundation of a house. You put in the foundation, build the house, and then sell more stuff. That's all you do.

You want to double your income? Talk to twice as many people as you're talking to today. The average salesperson, I have found, has no idea how many people they're talking to on a daily or weekly basis. If you say, talk to more people, they don't know how many people they're talking to today.

Go back to what I said before. Write things down. Track. Put things on paper and make a list. How many people did you speak to today? How many did you speak to yesterday? How many are you going to speak to tomorrow?

Keep your eye on the ball. The number of people that you speak to is going to determine the entire future of your business. People say, "I don't like to sell." People don't like to sell because they're not good at it. Why are they not good at it? They have not been trained in it.

When I first started in professional selling—business-to-business investment selling and real estate—I was nervous when I called on people. Then I realized I didn't know how to sell.

So I started to read and study and practice what I had learned in selling. I did it six days a week, for ten or twelve hours a day. If I was not working, I was learning.

Here's the number-three turning point. Number one: accept responsibility; no excuses. Number two: set goals. Write them down, make a list, and work on them. Number three: you can learn anything that you need to learn.

Once I realized that I needed to talk to more customers, I got better and better. The more time you spend talking to customers, the better you get at talking to customers. The less time it takes you to make a sale, the more your self-confidence increases. You're more eager to call on more people, because it increases your income and the quality of your life.

That's why successful people in MLM or in any other business are happy. They're happy because human beings are motivated by accomplishment. If they decide to make a sale and they make it, they're happy. They have more energy. They have more self-confidence. Their self-esteem is higher. They feel more valuable, and they're more eager to do more of the things that are making them feel good.

Sales is everything. The number-one reason for business success is high sales. The number-one reason for business problems is low sales. Everything else is commentary.

People say, "I don't have enough money." No—you're not making enough sales. Why not? You're not talking to enough people, and you're not asking them to buy your product. It's a simple thing.

"Yes, but the market is this, and the market is that." If what you say is true, then everybody will be failing, but if there are companies and businesses around you that are selling products and services, it means that perhaps this is a localized problem: you're simply not making enough calls on enough people, or the methods that you're using don't work.

I have a client who has been working for twelve years. He's built a very successful business, lives in a big home in an expensive neighborhood, drives an expensive car. But in the last twelve months, his sales have stopped.

It worked well for eleven years; his customers were good customers and provided him with a great living. But one by one, three major clients, whom he'd developed and matured, all quit. They said, "I don't want your services anymore."

"Why not?"

"I don't think they work."

So everything is, does it work? Will it get me the results that I want? The person buys the product because they're persuaded or convinced that it works.

Your job is to talk to more people and persuade them that your product or service will give them a result that they want, consistently and dependably. They'll come back and they'll buy over and over again. Never take your eye off the ball.

My business has gone up and down like a roller coaster. Whenever my business has gone down, I immediately say, "OK, time to get on the phone and make appointments and go and see people and talk to them and ask them to buy my product."

Don't buy more advertising, and no planning more promotions. Just get out there and talk to customers.

When I started off in sales, I knew that every businessperson earning a good living was a prospective customer for me. So I would say, who's your customer? Everybody is my customer. No, everybody may be a prospect, but they're not *your* prospect.

Some people are not your prospect. You are not at their social level, their income level, their educational level. You're not the kind of person who can meet them, greet them, talk to them. As you go through your day, you realize that everybody is a potential prospect, but they're not *your* potential prospect.

Every new product or service that comes out is a possible opportunity, but they're not always an opportunity *for you*. So you just keep trying different things.

A basic rule in statistics says that the more different things you try, the more information you gather, and the more you learn, the more likely you are to strike lightning—to find the product that's right for you. But you have to look at a lot of things; you have to try a whole lot of different things. You have to be prepared for the fact that there may be great product opportunities out there, but they're not all for you.

You keep expanding the number of different products and services and opportunities that you're looking at. As you expand them, you will find the one that is absolutely right. Many people, as I've pointed out, will stumble into a product or service combination that's different from what they ever thought, but it causes lightning to strike.

Suddenly, because of all the research and homework they've done up until then, everything comes together in that moment, and they'll have a product like a Krispy Kreme donut, which is so delicious. Your job is to find a product or service that's delicious, that people want and need and enjoy, and when they buy it, they say, "This is really great. I want to get this again and again."

The best entrepreneurs are the ones who are the most ambitious, the most aggressive. They try the most things. They experiment the most. They look at ways of taking something that may be good and making it even better, and then making it really excellent.

4

Essential #2
How Should I Finance
My Business?

When you start off as an entrepreneur, you tend to be overoptimistic. You think, "This is a great product or service. I'm going to sell truckloads of it, and I'm going to make an enormous amount of money." Then you have a shock. Your initial shock is how hard it is to sell a new product for the first time to a customer, how hard it is to get a customer to buy from you when they're quite satisfied with that they are already using, or they're not using this kind of product at all.

You think it's a very logical thing to choose your product, but they have no interest in it at all. "I'm not interested. I don't want it. I can't see how it can improve my life or work."

The number-one reason companies have trouble is they run out of cash, and the reason they run out of cash is that they don't have enough sales. The reason they don't have enough sales is that they have not thought through the product or service—who is going to buy it, why they would buy it, how much they would pay, or how it will be produced and delivered.

These are all elements of a business plan, which forces you to think through these elements before committing your resources. You know the old story about the guy who's driving through the country, and he's lost. He stops by a farmer and says to him, "Look, I'm trying to get to this particular place from here." The farmer sits there for a while and thinks and says, "Well, sir, you can't get there from here."

It's a funny little remark, yet many people start off with the idea of starting a business, but they can't get there from here for a variety of reasons. When I started my business (and I've started several), I found that the critical thing is cash, and cash comes from making sales. The number-one reason companies of all sizes fail is they deviate from this focus on generating cash. Then you have to borrow it. You have to beg, borrow, and steal. This is why the question, "How should I finance my business?" is an essential part of your success.

I sometimes joke that when I started my speaking and consulting business, I learned how to sell again. I sold my house, I sold my car, and I sold my furniture. I moved to rented premises. I had to park my car a block away so it didn't get picked up by the bank. When I continued to

The number-one reason companies have trouble is that they run out of cash, and the reason they run out of cash is that they don't have enough sales.

run out of money, I started to go to my friends with a cup in hand. I went to my younger brother, who was not very successful at all, and had to borrow from him just to stay alive. Then I had to go to friends that I'd met in business and ask for money as well. I had to borrow against everything and sell everything. As we said before, it was almost like being an airplane in a dive—running out of money.

I learned later that there are certain qualities that are essential for success in business, and one of them is the ability to manage money. It's your ability to accumulate it, to save it, to dispense with it, to use it intelligently, and to create more money. Most people start off without that ability, and that's what happened with me.

For the first two to four years of your new business, you're racing against time. You're struggling, you're striving. Nobody believes how hard it's going to be at the beginning, because you simply don't have the skills. Most entrepreneurs, the 80/20, quit after the first one or two or three years, because they don't have the persistence to hang in there through all the disappointments.

Sometimes people have a home, and they have to sell it all and go hat in hand and borrow from everybody. Sometimes they go completely broke. This is why banks will never lend you money. This is why no venture capitalist with half a brain will lend you money, because the failure rate is 99 percent. You have not demonstrated an ability to acquire money, deploy that money, and turn it into more money, so you have to exchange financial equity with sweat equity—you have to work and work. If you keep working away, reading and learning and studying and going everywhere that you can for ideas and information and help and support, eventually, if you're fortunate, you turn the corner.

That's why 90 percent of businesses started by people with business experience succeed, and 80 percent of businesses started by people with no business experience fail: they don't know what they're doing. They especially don't know how to combine products, services, people, offices, facilities, and resources in a product that customers will pay more for than the total cost of providing the product. If you can do that, then you can take that money and reinvest it and do it again and again and again.

I've mentioned the importance of bootstrapping. Bootstrapping forces you to become very smart very fast, because if you don't, you'll be out of business.

Business planning is one of the greatest insurance policies. Business planning forces you to think through every aspect of your business before you begin. Very often you will find that you can't get there from here. You have this idea for a product or service, but by the time you have carefully studied how much it's going to cost to produce it, import it, manufacture it, and distribute it, you'll have found that there are competitors who sell the same product, or a very similar one, for less money, and they already have a reputation.

One question you always ask is, why would somebody switch from their current supplier of a product or service to me, a brand-new, unknown quantity? Human beings like security, and they like assurance. Human beings are skeptical and careful. They don't want to lose money. Therefore you're going to have to provide a real advantage in order to make a person switch from whatever they're doing now to buying from you.

The great examples of this are the business legends. For example, Apple will be taught and discussed in schools. They came out with an idea. They'd never even been in the business of telephones, and they came up with an idea of a new phone, a totally different approach to telephone communications.

Of course their competitors said, "It's a toy; they're wasting their time. Nobody's going to switch from the established model of the cell phone to something completely unknown, where you have a single button, and everything is done on a single screen." But Apple had the confidence to push forward and bring this phone to market. People tried it, and they liked it. It was a quantum leap ahead of anything that was out there. Within five years, they'd transformed the world's telephone market, and all their major competitors were gone.

Tom Peters wrote a book some years ago called *In Search of Excellence*. It was the first business book that was on *The New York Times* best-seller list for months. He had eight principles that were essential for business success.

Peters was asked, "What is the most important of all these principles?" He said that the most important principle is an obsession with customer service, an obsession with taking care of customers. It's making sales and then taking care of those customers so they buy again.

Every single company that's successful, going back hundreds of years all the way up to today, has a reputation for offering excellent products and services and then taking really good care of their customers, almost obsessively.

It's very simple to do, but it's so easy to become distracted. It's so easy to be busy with your meetings and your coffee and your online programs and all kinds of little things that you get distracted from selling.

How much time do people in the average company spend actually selling the product? It works out to about ninety minutes a day. The rest of the time, they're busy getting started and winding up and winding down and talking to people and meeting people for lunch.

There's a firm that's worked with more than 6,000 companies in trouble. They tell them, "We can turn your company around, and we're going to charge you for it." It's astonishing how many will say, "No, we don't want to pay to have our company turned around. We're struggling at this level of sales."

The consultant's hardest job is to convince the owner of the company that he should hire them and pay them a

---

"The most important principle for business success
is an obsession of customer service, an obsession
with taking care of customers."
—Tom Peters, author of *In Search of Excellence*

---

reward for saving his company. The ones that do save the company. They always know what the problem is. It's that the head of the company is spending too much time doing things that are not sales. They're playing golf during the week. They're visiting with their friends. They're going for lunch. They're doing all kinds of big-shot things.

This firm goes in there, and they are as hard as nails. They say, "Stop this stuff, and get back to selling from first thing in the morning to the last thing at night. Focus 100 percent on your customers." Over and over again, they turn the company around.

Your job as a business owner, as an entrepreneur is to think about customers and talk about customers and talk to customers. You become obsessed with customer service. That'll be about 90 percent of your success.

Peter Drucker says that the most important number in business is free cash flow. Free cash flow is the amount of cash that you generate after all activities, after all costs, after everything. How much money do you have in your hand at the end of the day that you can put in your pocket and walk away with?

That's the most important number of all, for a shoeshine boy on a corner and for General Motors and the biggest companies. Always free cash flow. I've worked with more than a thousand of the biggest companies in the world. They're all the same. The successful companies are all focused on customers and sales. Every single day, it's customer and sales. All rewards, all promotions, all benefits, all growth comes back to customers and sales.

The least successful companies are ones that get distracted. They get distracted with new product design and new offices. The best example I think is the dot-com, dot-bomb activities that took place in the nineties. All of these companies were being started, and they were investing enormous amounts of other people's money. They had this idea that if you invest in my company, we'll have a new product or service that nobody else has ever had before, and people are just going to show up at our website in droves, and you're going to make a jillion dollars. We all know how that story turned out for too many of those early Internet companies. The dot-coms that survived and thrived decided to invest in brand building.

Brand building is one of the most powerful things you can do. This is where customers know that if I buy your product or service, I'm going to have this benefit or advantage. You have a reputation.

The Harvard Business School said that your reputation is your most valuable business asset. Your products and services will come and go. Your people will come and go. Your competition will come and go, but your reputation for the quality and value of your product or service stays constant.

Companies will often buy another company, which may have a value of a million dollars. The company will pay $10 million for it. What's the other $9 million for? It's called *goodwill*. Goodwill is actually a number on the books. Companies that have goodwill, which is reputation, are vastly more valuable than companies that don't.

"Your reputation is your most valuable business asset."
—Lesson from *The Harvard Business School*

Every single customer interaction has to increase goodwill. It has to cause people to like you, because if you have a great reputation, it will shorten the amount of time it will take for a person to buy your product.

People buy iPhones automatically. They walk into the store and pay twice as much as for a competing product. Apple keeps raising the prices, and they don't discount. The reason is their reputation. "Oh, it's an Apple. It's the best in the business. If it's the best in the business, I will pay a premium price for it, and I will buy it again and again and again." People line up around the block to buy the product because of the reputation. The reputation is the focus on customer service and on product quality.

If you are in business at any level, there are four key questions you have to ask and answer over and over again. Customers, investors, contributors do not ask these questions clearly or out loud, but you still have to answer them.

Four Key Questions for Investors
1. How much in?
2. How much out?
3. How quick?
4. How sure?

The first question is, *how much in?* How much do you want me to put in to your business venture? Question number two is, *how much out?* How much am I going to get back?

I'm working on a large real-estate development right now, and I'm speaking with my partners. We're going back and forth, and I explained this to them: your proposal, your pro forma, your business plan, your investment offering has to ask those two questions. How much in, how much out?

The third question is, *how fast?* How soon will I get my money back? The fourth question is, *how sure?* How can I be guaranteed?

If your answer to any one of those is not satisfactory, the person will not invest. They will just say, "I'll pass. Let me think about it. I'm not interested. It's not a good idea this time."

I've spoken to thousands of entrepreneurs. They all had the same concern: how hard it is to get people to part with their money, how hard it is to answer those four questions. People will grind you on those answers. It can't be a general "Oh, you'll make a lot of money. You're going to make a lot of money hand over fist."

To go back to the dot-coms, people were putting in hundreds of millions, even billions of dollars into these half-baked ideas. They called them "prerevenue companies." A prerevenue company is a company that has never made a sale, and people were actually paying enormous amounts of money for these companies.

Today it's different. Mark Zuckerberg paid billions of dollars for Instagram before they'd even made a sale, and

---

4 Silent Questions Every Potential Investor Asks Themselves:

1. How much in?   3. How fast?
2. How much out?   4. How sure?

---

people said, "This is crazy. They never made a sale." He said, "Look at the numbers." They looked at the number of people who signed onto Instagram and who as a result signed on to Facebook. Then they looked at the amount that these people would buy, invest, and spend on advertising products and services and how much other people would pay to get them as potential customers.

Today, with Zuckerberg and Facebook, all their money is coming from selling advertising to people who want to access to companies like Instagram. They will pay a fortune, hundreds of dollars per name, because over time those people will spend an enormous of money on products for years. That's why you see these crazy numbers today.

They tried the same thing back in the nineties, and most of them failed. My business partner today was the head of one of these pre-revenue companies, and they had 600 staff; 600 staff members working like fanatics twelve, fourteen, sixteen hours a day—coming in early, and staying late all week. They spent hundreds of millions of dollars, took office buildings, but before the dust settled, they lost everything, and they never made a sale. It's because they didn't realize how hard it is to answer the four questions: How much in? How much out? How fast? How sure?

In business-to-business selling, in anything that has to do with investments and development or growth, those questions come up over and over. If you want someone to give you money for your business, you need to ask, how much do you want them to give you, what will they get back, when will they get it back, and how sure can they be?

How much in? How much out? How fast? How sure? People don't ask these questions aloud. But they think these questions, and even though sometimes they're unclear in their minds, those questions have to be answered. If you don't answer them to the satisfaction of the person whose money you want, they will say no.

I'm working with my development right now, which embraces about $380 million worth of commercial property in a very fast-growing area of the United States. I sat down with my partners for three or four days, and we went back and forth. How much in? How much out?

They said, "It's going to be really good." I said, "No, no that's not enough. It has to be very, very clear, specific, written down, and you have to prove it. What are the numbers exactly? What are the rental rates that are available? What are the number of prospective tenants in this area? How much will they pay? How soon will they pay it? How quickly will they take occupancy?"

How much in? How much out? How fast? How sure? Now my partners—who are some of the smartest development people in the United States, based in New York, with thirty, forty years' experience—think in terms of the four questions. In every second email, we talk about them.

We've improved the answer to question number three. We're working on question number two, and so on.

You need to do the same thing. In business, money is a very hard thing. It's not soft and wishy-washy—"Oh, it'll be great." Too many people, including you and me, have lost too much money by investing in pie in the sky. Now we won't do it. If we have any temptation to invest in pie in the sky, our friends, our spouses, our business partners, will slap us down and stop us. They'll ask us hard, steely questions. They're cold and unemotional, and we need to be the same way to invest money.

Remember I said before that everyone wants expediency. Everyone wants to improve their condition. Everyone wants to earn more money and have more money. Everyone wants to be financially independent and possibly rich. So there's always money available for your good idea. If you build it, they will come—the *Field of Dreams* movie.

One of the most famous lines for 150 years in American business was, "If you build a better mousetrap, the world will beat a path to your door." That was perhaps true at a very early stage of American business, but not anymore. If you build a better mousetrap, you're going to have to beat a path to the customer's door, and you're going to have to line up, and you're going to have to go back and see them over and over again. Some of the greatest investment successes were a result of somebody going back over and over again, week after week, month after month, year after year. Whether it's a bank, a capitalist, a friend, or an angel investor, they sometimes take a long time to be convinced that the return is sure enough to give it a try.

Angel investors, by the way, are one of the most popular types of investors. These are people who have earned a lot of money in business. They want to earn more, but they don't want to start a business themselves, so they'll invest in new up-and-coming companies. They'll not only take an equity interest, but they'll also add their expertise. These people have made a lot of money starting and building one or more businesses, so they will contribute a certain amount of money in exchange for your using their expertise and ability. That's one good source.

Author W. Clement Stone once said that if you cannot save money, the seeds of greatness are not in you. You have to be able, at an early age, to practice self-sacrifice, self-discipline, self-mastery. You have to restrict your expenditures. You have to save money.

If you cannot save money and have to go to someone hat in hand saying, "I have this business idea, but I have no money," the potential investor, if they have half a brain, will not give you any money either, because you have demonstrated that you do not have the ability to handle money, just like a child with an allowance who goes out and buys candy.

I learned this about self-made millionaires. They don't buy new cars. Why? Because if you buy a quality used car and take the rest of the money and invest that in your business or property, then it can grow. Therefore they don't buy new cars. They buy used things.

When you're starting a new business—and I made every single one of these mistakes—people rent new offices and buy new furniture. They buy new technology, equipment, information, computers. Successful people buy used, or they borrow, or they rent, or they lease. They just keep cutting down cash outgo. As a result, they demonstrate that they are capable of having money.

Many years ago, I was given a business to start and operate by my big boss. He's an entrepreneur. He owns 200 companies, and he was brought a new business, and he turned to me and said, "What do you think of this business?"

I said, "Let me do some research," and I did. I came back in about two weeks with a complete, detailed business plan that said that this was a good business; it had great potential. He said, "All right. I'll put you in charge of it, and I'll give you a percentage of the profits."

So he did, and I went to work on this business. I knew nothing about this business. Importation and distribution. I worked and worked for twelve, fifteen hours a day. I had black patches under my eyes for two or three years because I worked seven days a week to make this successful, and I finally did.

I had to have a distribution warehouse with offices. So I found a renovated warehouse that had been in an old manufacturing part of town. I rented these offices, and then I went to a couple of auctions where they had business furniture, chairs, shelving, and things like that for sale. I bought it all used. For me, it seemed like the logical thing to do. If you buy it brand-new, you can pay two, three, or four times as much than if you bought used stuff at auctions from companies that went broke.

After about six or eight months, the company was up and running. It was starting to generate sales and profits. The big boss lived in a distant city. He came up for the first time to look at the business, and he walked around the business, and there's my staff, and there's the offices. We had very small offices.

He said, "I'm quite amazed that you have been so cheap with everything that you do. What I have learned is small expenses mean high profits." Without him lecturing to me, I automatically looked for every conceivable way to save money. He was surrounded by people in his businesses who were throwing money away buying new cars and new furniture and new offices, whereas I was cheap, cheap, cheap, and I turned that company into $25 million of profits within twenty-four months. It was one of the most profitable divisions of his worldwide companies. The resentment from the other people in the other companies was incredible, but I kept focusing on two things. Keep the cost down, and focus on sales and do nothing but sales, sales, sales.

The formula was phenomenal, and I learned that in my thirties. It opened up every other door for me. My boss gave me another business opportunity, another company to start and to build from scratch, and then another, and soon I was running three divisions of this multinational company. Each division was making profits, and why? Because of a very simple focus. Keep the cost down and focus on sales.

It's one of the most important principles in life: if you demonstrate that you can do well with small opportunities, every door will open for you, but if you can't demonstrate that, if you can't get results, if you can't generate profits at a small level, all doors will remain closed. Nothing will happen, and you'll go back to working for wages.

If you can demonstrate that you can do well with small opportunities, every door will open for you.

5

Essential #3
Shifting from an Employee Mindset to an Entrepreneurial Mindset

Now that you've gotten started, how do shift your mentality from the perspective of someone who works for wages to that of an entrepreneur?

This is the third essential element for entrepreneurial success: It's the mentality of "no entitlement" that is more typical of the entrepreneur, versus "entitlement" which is often associated with the employee. If you are to start and succeed in your own business, you must embrace this concept: *Nobody owes you anything.* As I keep saying, people love security, and they love to be safe. So companies artfully offer them security in exchange for lower income. You can hire a person who generates a certain amount of revenue from their activities, and you can pay them—the rule is no more than a third of the revenue they generate, but better a sixth, and better a tenth.

Look at a company like Microsoft. Today it has 120,000 employees, and it's one of the most profitable companies in the world, but every one of those people contributes more value than they cost, so every one of those people contributes a profit.

A good staff member is free plus a profit. That means that whatever you pay them, they're generating more revenue than it's costing you to keep them as employees. Therefore every additional person is an additional profit source, and some of them are extraordinary profit sources.

You take a man like Steve Ballmer, who went to college and then went to work for a large company, Procter & Gamble. He worked in a little cubicle, and from there he worked his way up until people around him realized, "This guy is a real producer. He earns money. If we put him in a position, no matter how much we pay him, we get far more return on it." So they gave him more jobs, more responsibility, more people. He eventually became the president of Microsoft, and when he retired, his Microsoft shares were worth $6.7 billion. And he started off as an employee generating revenue.

People go to work for other companies because they seek security more than opportunity, instead of really high income, which is possible if you go all in (as they say

A good staff member is free—plus a profit.

in Texas hold'em): if you're successful, you can make a lot of money. Instead they work for another company that gives them security and safety: medical care, savings plans, 401(k)s, and vacation days. One thing I say to my audiences is, "You and I are different from most people. We can only eat what we kill. If we don't make a sale, if we don't generate revenue, then we don't eat."

The number-one attitude for success in life, business, and entrepreneurship is self-responsibility. I mentioned earlier that discovering this changed my life forever. I realized that if I took charge of my own life, there was no limit to what I could do. I could learn any subject that I needed to learn to earn more money, as long as I had a clear goal or a business plan, which is a series of goals that overlap with each other. You go through life, and at a certain point you realize, "Hey, I'm responsible. I'm in charge of my own life. I can do whatever I want with my life as long as I don't make excuses."

A few years ago, I got a call from a publisher. The top people in the publishing house, one of the biggest in the country, had an editorial meeting and asked, "What's a good subject? What kinds of books are people buying today? We're always looking for a hit subject—something that potential customers really want and need and can benefit from."

They concluded that there was a big market for self-discipline. They knew me from the industry, so they called me up and said, "We think that you would be the best person to write a book on self-discipline. What do you think?"

"I have studied self-discipline since I was a young man," I said, "because self-discipline is self-mastery, self-control, self-responsibility. I love the subject, because it's so essential. It's the heartbeat of success. You never make excuses."

So I wrote a book called *No Excuses! The Power of Self-Discipline*. That book sells thousands of copies in twenty-five languages. Recently I was doing a teleconference in German. Two of the people held up their copies of the book in German. They were waving this book and had big smiles, and they said, "This book changed my life."

All over the world—no excuses. You don't waste a single minute of energy or anger or frustration when something doesn't work out. You say, "I am responsible." I think those words are magic. *I am responsible. I am responsible.* Like a drumbeat: *I am responsible.*

Your sales are down. Your income is down. You have financial problems. You hired a person, and the person turns out to be inappropriate, or a jerk. You got into a bad business deal. You lost your money.

You just say, "Wait a minute. I'm responsible." You don't blame the other person. You don't blame the situation. You don't blame the economy. You just keep saying, "I am responsible."

In the world today, especially in our country, you basically have two types of people. On the one hand are those who believe that others are responsible. If something is not going well for them, someone else is to blame. In fact, some political philosophies only exist so they can blame someone else for something that is wrong somewhere, somehow.

Then you have the other type of mentality, which is the self-responsible mentality. Now who do you think are the people who are the hardest-working, the most admired, the most respected, the leaders, the ones who are most successful over time? It's always the self-responsible people. You cannot imagine a successful person who blames all their problems on someone else.

There are people saying, "I should be paid twice as much as I'm being paid." On what basis? On what basis should you be paid more than you're getting today?

If you want to be paid more, just say, "I am responsible for increasing my value. I am responsible for doing a little more, starting a little earlier, staying a little later. If I do that, then I'll automatically be paid more. If I put more in, I'm going to get more out." It's called—going back to the Bible—the law of sowing and reaping. "Whatsoever a man soweth, that shall he reap." If you're not happy with what you are reaping today, then sow something more and different.

Self-responsibility is the starting point of successful entrepreneurship. Without it, nothing is possible. Self-responsibility is not enough to guarantee your success, but it is absolutely essential for success.

If you want to be paid more just say, 'I am responsible for increasing my value. I am responsible for doing a little more, starting a little earlier, staying a little later. If I put more in, then I am going to get more out.

Here we have to remember the expediency factor. I think it's one of the most important things to understand in the world. Human beings are always seeking faster, easier ways to get the things they want, with little or no concern for long-term consequences. People want to live, they want to socialize, they want to have a home, and they're always looking for ways to do it faster and more easily.

You have to discipline yourself to resist this natural tendency to do things more easily. As I've said, everything is hard before it's easy, and new habits are hard before they're easy.

Many years ago, I developed a system called the 1,000 percent formula. I practiced it myself year after year, and I began to teach it to other people. It's very simple.

How do you increase your income by 1,000 percent? The formula says this: if you increase your income by 25 percent per year, then you will, by compounding, increase your income ten times in ten years. How do you increase your income by 25 percent per year? You increase your productivity by 2 percent per month, by starting earlier, working harder, staying later, upgrading your skills, focusing on your most important activities.

If you do these things over and over again, at the beginning you see very little change. It's just like the old story: if you took a penny and you doubled the penny every day for a month, what difference would it make in your life? The answer is that a penny doubled every day for a month would be several million dollars, because of compounding.

If a person doubled a penny every single day for fifteen days, what would it be worth? It would be worth only a few dollars, but if it keeps doubling for twenty, twenty-five, thirty days—the amount is phenomenal. In farming, a kernel of wheat doubled every single day for six months would be all the food in the world.

With my 1,000 percent formula, I say the starting point of success is to get up early and exercise, physically exercise to get yourself moving, and then to read for thirty to sixty minutes each day in your field to improve your skills.

Surprise, surprise—early to bed, early to rise. Wealthy people get up before 6:00 a.m. In general, probably 80 percent of wealthy people get up before 6:00 a.m. My goal is to get up at two minutes to 6:00, one minute to 6:00. I have a clock sitting there. I stretch it out as much as possible, but if wealthy people get up at 6:00 a.m. and start their day, then I'm going to do the same thing.

Successful business people get up earlier. They have done as much work as the average person does in a day before the average person starts work. Wealthy people get up at 6:00. They have their whole day planned by 7:00. They hit the ground running by 8:00, and they have accomplished more by 10:00 or 11:00 than the average person accomplishes in an entire day.

The second thing is to plan every day in advance. Every single day, make a list in advance of everything that you have to do. That takes less than ten minutes. However, if you plan every day in advance, you will double your productivity in a very short period of time, because you save so much time by planning. You don't waste time. Then set priorities on your tasks. Everybody who practices these skills ends up increasing their productivity and their output by 2 percent a month, 25 percent a year. It just accumulates, it just marches and marches and marches.

When I started doing this way back in the seventies, I sat down and asked, "What things could you do that would increase your productivity?" One was continuous learning. The cumulative results were phenomenal. As I said, you could increase your income ten times in ten years.

Most of the people who have been through this little formula increase their income ten times in six or seven years. People come back to me from all over the world and say, "It doesn't take ten years to increase your income ten times. It's takes six, seven, eight years"—even faster for some.

I did it in five years, and I could not believe it. I was earning more than I'd ever dreamed, and it was gradual, cumulative. I decided I would do it again, and in the next five years I increased my income another ten times. I increased my income by 100 times in ten years and never went back.

If you can discipline yourself to upgrade your skills, to plan your day, to organize, to work harder, if you can discipline yourself so this becomes automatic every day, the cumulative effect is amazing. It becomes automatic, and you never go back down.

There are stories about people who become wealthy and start big businesses. Then there's a recession. They're over-leveraged, they've borrowed too much, spent too much, and they lose it all. There's an English developer who's quite outspoken. When the recession came a few years ago, he went from $350 million in net worth to zero, to living in the back bedroom of his friend's place. He didn't even have a home. People were asking, "What about your money?" "It's all gone. I don't have any money." Today he's coming back up again. He's worth $200 million, and why? It's because he keeps doing the things he did to make the money in the first place.

If one of your goals is to be wealthy, the first thing you do is study what wealthy people do. Wealthy people get up early. Wealthy people read an hour a day in their field to upgrade their skills. Wealthy people plan their days very carefully. Wealthy people attend seminars and workshops and conferences; they interact with other people and ask them for their ideas.

This is what wealthy people do, and you just get into the habit. You breathe in, you breathe out. You keep using your time efficiently, and you become better and better at what you do. You don't see any difference in the beginning, but the cumulative effect is like losing weight. If you lose an ounce a day, a little bit at a time, again it accumulates over time. Over the period of a year, two years, three years, you're at your perfect weight.

The difference is extraordinary as long as you are self-disciplined and you accept responsibility. You say that you're going to do it, and then you do it.

If one of your goals is to be wealthy, the first
thing you do is study what wealthy people do.

Networking is one of the most powerful techniques for rapid growth. People say that your income will be the average income of the five people with whom you spend the most time.

If you want to be successful, get around successful people. Ask a lot of questions. Take notes, because it could just be one thing that someone throws out at lunch or dinner or coffee: later you go back and look at it, and it contains a gem that can save you a week or a year of hard work.

I'm constantly gathering new ideas, new information. I work as a speaker and guide, but also as a coach. I coach people who quite commonly are worth hundreds of millions of dollars—some are even billionaires. They pay me for my services, and I charge a lot. I guarantee it: if you're not happy with the session we spend together—I usually do two-hour sessions, either phone or Skype, sometimes worldwide—then there's no charge. You don't have to pay.

I never have people ask for refunds, but I do have people say, "This session has changed my life. This session has changed my business. I had never heard that idea. I had never heard that insight. I had never seen that before. Where did you come up with that idea?" I say, "I really don't know, except that I just keep reading and learning and writing things down."

I talked a little bit earlier about writing things down. Think on paper. Your likelihood of remembering something goes up by 1,000 percent if you write it down. There are some great studies described in *The New York Times*, *Forbes*, and *The Wall Street Journal* where they looked at the difference between students at universities who take

Your likelihood of remembering something
goes up by 1,000 percent if you write it down.

notes and those who don't. Most students—80/20—don't take notes. They coast. They go to school, they listen to the professor speaking, and they jot a couple of notes down, but mostly they're on their iPhones or checking their computers or talking to their friends. The other students, the top 20 percent, write everything down. These students get top grades. If you write it down, then you remember it more.

In a couple of studies, they took a university class, and at the end of a session they did a quick exam. Everybody got the same grades, whether or not they took notes. But after the final exam, they found that the ones who had taken the most detailed notes got the top grades, whereas the others faded away. The difference was that the others had the notes to refer to.

I used to write notes in spiral notebooks. I'd carry them with me, and I was always writing notes from every class, every course, every seminar, everything. I now have filing cabinets full of notes, hundreds, probably millions of words, and if there was a really important book or subject, I would have page after page and notebook after notebook of notes.

When you write things down, you can refer back to them, but you also remember them at a deeper and deeper level. So the bottom line is, take notes. I joke that I don't even go to the bathroom without a pen and paper in my hand. If the phone rings, I grab something to write with before I answer the phone. If I'm going to a meeting, it's almost like a religion for me: I immediately grab something to write with so that I can capture it.

Countless times in my work, I will talk to a client, and I'll write down everything. I may not work with that client for a year or nine months. When I'm going to be addressing the top management of a big company or hundreds or thousands of people from large corporations, I go back to my notes. Even though I haven't looked at the notes for months, I have them. I have every single thing that we talked about, which I use to incorporate into speaking, teaching, and seminars.

They're astonished. They say, "We have not spoken about this for a year, and your seminar was exactly spot-on, word-for-word what we talked about." That's because I took good notes.

6

Essential #4
Creating a Realistic
Business Plan

Now that we've dealt with the essential concept of our internal mindset, it's time to cover some of the essential external tools used to ensure that a business will be a success story and not an unfortunate statistic. Essential #4 is to create and execute a realistic and productive business plan.

I teach a program called the Two-Day MBA. I condense the most important business ideas into two days. It's highly interactive; people transform their businesses and lives with questions. I learned decades ago that the most important part of thinking is asking good questions,

questions that are called *proactive*—you provoke your very best thinking by asking really good questions.

One reason people say to me, "You changed my life, you changed my career, you changed everything" is the questions. "I never heard that question before. This forced me to answer the question, and when I came up with the answer, which I hadn't thought about before, it transformed everything."

Questions for Business Plans

1. What is the product to be sold? What difference will it make in the customer's life?
2. Who is the ideal customer?
3. What value does the customer seek? What is the problem to be solved?
4. How is the product to be sold?
5. Who is going to sell the product?
6. How much will you charge for the product?
7. How will the product be produced?
8. How will the product be delivered?
9. How will the customer be charged?
10. How will the product be installed?
11. How will the customer be serviced?
12. Who will do all these jobs?

In a business plan, there are really three big questions and several others. It all begins with, why do people buy anything? The answer, which I learned in studying economics many years ago, is that human action is always inspired

> Human action is always inspired
> by the desire for improvement.

by the desire for improvement. Whatever your product or service is, people will buy it to improve the conditions of their life in some way.

Similarly, people will not act unless they feel that by taking action they are going to improve their conditions. A prospective customer is a customer who is dissatisfied. We call that a *felt dissatisfaction*. The person in some way is not happy with their existing condition. You offer a product or service that will take away that dissatisfaction in a cost-effective manner.

The first question is, *what is the product to be sold and what difference will it make in the customer's life*? You have to get right back down to the psychology and the basic economics of why people act. People do not buy products or services. Again, sometimes I joke with my audiences. I say, "I have interviewed your customers and prospective customers in this market, and I have found that none of them care about your product or service or your company or your business or anything else. Nobody cares about what you sell. To them, it's completely irrelevant. They only care about one thing: What does the product or service do? How does the product or service change my life or my work or my family in some way?"

That answer must be crystal-clear, or people will simply dismiss you. What does your product or service do to change the life or work of your prospective customer?

My favorite word in business is *clarity*. I designed my business-coaching program some years ago, and I spoke of the *focal point*. A focal point is that point where, when you hold a magnifying glass at the right angle, the rays of the sun burn through.

The ability to focus on one thing at a time is the absolutely essential skill for success, especially to focus on improving the life or work of your customers in some way. In a business plan, question number one is, what is the product to be sold?

You always define your product in terms of the difference it will make in the life of the customer. How will the customer's life be changed or different afterwards? You must be crystal-clear about that, because if the customer's not crystal-clear, they'll immediately dismiss your offering, and nothing will happen.

The second question in your business plan is, *who is the ideal customer*? In business planning, the two big questions are "What is my product?" and "Who is my customer?" What and who? What is my product, and who is my customer? Of all the customers, who is the ideal customer, the perfect customer?

I read a book some years ago, and there was one point in it that was worth the entire price, and it was called *finding perfect customers*. What is it that you offer that causes you to deserve, to attract perfect customers? What is it that you offer? You want perfect customers. Well, how do you deserve them? What is it that you do that justifies people buying from you?

Focus on that all the time, justifying perfect customers, so that what you offer is superior to anything else that your competitors will offer. If you can do that, you're going to build a big, successful business, and you're going to be wealthy. Successful companies organize everything in their business to deserve to have perfect customers buy their product, and buy it again and again, and tell their friends.

So what is the product to be sold in terms of the difference it makes in the customer's life, and who's the ideal customer? This comes back to my word: *clarity, clarity, clarity.* What is their age? What is their education? What is their background? What is their current situation? What do they need and want? What do they worry about? What problems, goals, difficulties do they have?

You must be crystal-clear. In one exercise we give to our students, we say, "In the next break that's coming up, imagine that you're talking to someone. The person says, 'I know a lot of people in this city. I've been here for most of my life, and I probably know people who would be great customers for you.' So please describe to me your perfect customer, but do not tell me about your product or your service or your company or your business or anything else. It's almost like a mystery. It's almost like it's a secret quiz. Just tell me how you would describe your perfect customer, and I'll think of who fits that description."

You have to say who your ideal customer is, and what your ideal customer considers value. What does my ideal customer want so much that they will give me money for it? Remember, the customer is always right. If the customer says no, or if the customer hesitates, or the customer delays purchasing your product, they are telling you that you have come to the market with a wrong product.

Today many successful businesses are picking what they call an *avatar*, which is a perfect customer. They go out into the marketplace, and they find 1 or 10 or 20 or 100 people, and they'll work with them arm in arm, hand in hand to develop a product that these people love. This is the perfect product.

One example is a gentleman who built a very successful high-tech company and sold it for millions of dollars, and he decided to do it again. This is what successful people do: they start a company, they build it up, they generate a high cash flow, they sell it, and they do it again. They find another product, a new service, a new customer market.

This man's team spent millions of dollars and more than a year working in private to develop this product, which they thought was great. Then they had a big debate inside the company: should we release a beta model free so that people can give us their opinion, try it out, and tell us what they want more of or less of, or should we go to market with a product for sale?

The common way products are sold today is that the product simply appears in the market, especially in stores. You go to the store, and suddenly there it is. You have no warning at all, no idea that the product is coming. They want to keep it secret, because they don't want their competitors to steal the march on them.

So this company said, "We'll take 10,000 prospective customers on our databases, and we'll offer the product for free."

They sent it out, and they offered it for free. They were all waiting for feedback—what people liked, and what they didn't like, and so on. To their astonishment, there was complete silence. They didn't get any reaction. They're sitting there. They've spent millions of dollars, and they offered it for free, and there's no reaction.

The president of the company did something he had never done before in his work in high-tech. (Tech people don't like to talk to customers. They like to do everything online.) He got the phone number of one of the customers on the database. He phoned him and asked, "We sent you a free offer to take this product at no charge at all, and we noticed that you didn't respond to the offer. Could you tell us why not?"

The customer said, "Because I don't want the product."

"But it's free."

"I don't want it for free."

The people in this company—engineers, techies, product developers—thought this product was as hot as a firecracker; people would be tearing it out of their hands. But they said, "I don't want it at any price."

"You don't want it any price?"

"No. This does not satisfy any need I have. It does not solve a problem. It does not overcome an obstacle. It does not improve my life in any way."

The president of the company was shocked, so he asked the customer, "What is it that you want?"

"I certainly don't want this, but it does have a couple of good features, and if you offered this and this in conjunction with this, then I would be really interested in it."

So the company went back and changed the product. The customers said, "It's still pretty good, but I don't have time for it," and they still wouldn't take it even for free. The company went back ninety-nine times to their database and kept offering it and asking for feedback. After ninety-nine times, it was a completely different product. Everybody they offered it to was so excited that they bought it by the truckloads. It became a multimillion-dollar product. The people in the company said, "The shocker for us was to actually pick up the phone and ask the customer's opinion before we launched the product." This is important today. The companies that are really successful are those that are doing a lot of preparation in advance.

One of my favorite stories is about a major pet-food company that invested $350 million to create the perfect dog food. Nutritionally—protein, minerals, vitamins—it's the most perfect dog food that's ever been invented. They developed it in secret and launched it nationwide, and sales were flat. They asked what happened. Why were there no sales?

The response was, "The product is perfect on paper, but the dogs hate it." This is a great example: the dogs hate it. Before your launch, you have to make sure that the prospective customers love it.

The third question: *what value does the customer seek?* What is it that would cause a person to give one of the following three responses? You say, "Here is my value offering." The first response is "I want that," and it must be knee-jerk, like a switchblade. People don't have to think or make notes on paper. You say, "Here's the value offering," and the person says, "I want that."

The second reaction is, "That's for me. I want it *now*, and I don't even care about the price. I just want that benefit that's going to change or improve my life in some way."

The third reaction is, "How do you do that?" Worldwide, the most popular and successful single advertisement that you can publish is "Save money on your taxes." You place that ad, and the eyes of anybody who is reading the newspaper will shoot to it, because every single person feels they're paying too much in taxes. They're getting over-taxed, they get few benefits for those taxes, and of course they *hate* to pay taxes.

So how can you design your value offering in such a way that it unconsciously triggers, "I want that." "That's for me." "How do you do that?" One of those three, and if you do that, you have a winner. If your advertising line doesn't trigger that reaction, you have to go back to the drawing board. The customer is always right. The customer always knows what is exactly right for him or her at this time, and your job is to conform to that. Your job is *not* to convince or persuade the customer to buy it.

Design your value offering in such a way
that it unconsciously triggers, "I want that."
"That's for me." "How do you do that?"

This is an essential part of the business plan. The more you test it in advance, the more likely it is that you're going to get the right answer, that you're going to bring the right product or service to market, that you're going to make sales very quickly, and that you're going to be successful as an entrepreneur. The flip side is that if you don't get these positive reactions, your product or service will fail.

The more time you spend thinking in advance and getting your business plan right, the more likely your business is to be successful. You have a product or a service that people want and need and are willing to pay for. Now how are you going to sell it? That's what caused all of the dot-coms to collapse: they were all started by people who were techies who had never sold anything.

Companies started by entrepreneurs, who had to sell something from the first day to stay alive, are completely different from companies that are run by someone who did not start the company, because the person now in charge never had to sell to survive at the beginning. Their whole mentality is different. It's worst of all if a family member who has never had any sales experience is put in charge of a company.

This is an entrepreneurial company. It's working in a very busy, dynamic, aggressive market, where you have to be constantly offering products and services faster, better, cheaper, and so on just to stay alive, and you're constantly changing them. Because the selling process is the turning point. It's the axle. It's the focal point of the entire business process.

When small companies start off, they throw themselves at the market like a dog chasing a passing car. They're exhausted. They spent all their resources to finally get a sale of some kind, whereas companies, as they grow, pull back and say, "We need a sales system."

So instead of having every salesperson selling differently, the company develops a sales system. This is what made IBM the biggest computer company in the world, also many companies like Hewlett-Packard and Google and Apple. Every successful company develops a system, like McDonald's or any franchise. You buy the proven system, you learn the system, and you do not deviate from the system. The company is set up in such a way that when you phone for information, you'll get a message saying, "This call will be monitored for quality control." They're going to check to make sure that whomever you're speaking to is saying the same thing. If you call the company in a different time and a different place and speak to a different person, they'll all say the same thing.

That's when companies explode. They develop a system that works, and it multiplies. Like the example of this person running a shipping company: he found that what he needed is more people saying the same thing to get customers to ship their furniture. Once they had a sales system and multiplied it, they didn't double their sales

---

To achieve explosive growth with your company,
spend the time and money to develop a system
that works. It will multiply your growth.

---

in five years, they increased it 106 times in five years, because all they had to do was hire and train more people.

I worked many years ago with an encyclopedia sales company. These are companies with salespeople that go from door to door and sell from house to house. When they recruited you, they said, "If you follow our system, you can earn $50,000 a year." Most of the people who were attracted to this were people with no money, limited education, no opportunities, and limited skills.

I stood back and watched the company at work. They could take a person and teach them, just like teaching them to memorize a poem or song. The person would memorize the sales presentation.

They'd spent a fortune developing this presentation. It had forty-two questions. You ask this, the customer says that. You ask this, the customer says that. If the customer says something different, you go back and you ask it again until the customer is saying yes, yes, yes.

The first question was, when the salesperson would come to the door, they would say, "Hello, I'm Brian Tracy with International Educational Systems. Do you live here? Is this your home?" They would always ask, "Is this your home?" because they'd found that sometimes the person was a visitor or a relative or a renter, and these people would not buy. They did not have the interest or the money, so salespeople had to start off with the right question: "Is this your home?"

The customer said, "This is my home."

"Great. Do you believe in the importance of higher education?"

The person would say yes. If a person said no, the salesperson would stop and walk away. If a person does not believe in higher education, there's no point in talking to them about purchasing a set of encyclopedias for higher education.

The company had forty-two questions like this that they had experimented with, and the forty-second was, "Can you press hard? There are two copies," and you'd make the sale. They sold a billion dollars' worth of encyclopedias with this. Every company stole it from Encyclopedia Britannica, which was the giant at the time. If you followed the system, and you asked the right questions, and people answered the questions in the proper way, you made jillions of dollars in sales.

So the best companies today, worldwide, have proven sales systems, and that's what makes them huge. However, 70 percent of companies, especially small companies, do no sales training at all. They hire people. They give them their brochures. They give them a little product knowledge and have a question-and-answer session about how the product works. They say, "What do you say when people say this?" and they say, "OK, that's great." And then you'll go out there and talk to people.

They don't understand why every month they're struggling to make payroll. They're struggling to have enough money to keep going until finally they develop a system. They take all the best knowledge that they have. They put it together, and everybody agrees to follow this system word-for-word. The sales go up ten times.

The fourth question is *how is the product to be sold*? This is not a random question. This is like, if you need brain surgery or heart surgery to live, how is this surgery to be done? You don't want to say, "Oh, don't worry about that. Get a couple of scalpels in the operating theater." No, this is the critical part of the operation.

The fifth question is *who is going to sell the product*? Who specifically is going to interact face-to-face, one-to-one—we say head-to-head, knee-to-knee—with the prospect to make this sale?

Again, you'll find that your best companies are extremely careful about this question. They think it through in advance. Who is it going to be? How are they going to dress? How are they going to look? What are they going to say? What are they going to do before and after the meeting? What's the process?

To find and hire a good salesperson is one of the hardest things in the world. It's easier to get a brain surgeon or a heart surgeon. It's easier to get almost any other kind of skilled individual than a really good salesperson.

Here's a big mistake. People are always trying to save money by paying salespeople as little as possible. They're complaining, "If I want to hire a good salesperson away from another company, they cost too much. You have to pay them."

Remember, a good salesperson is free plus a profit. They contribute far more in revenues and ultimately in profit than you pay them. I've spoken to people specializing in personnel selection. The smartest thing that you can do, if you're going to start a business, is to go out and pay anything that is required to get a super salesman or super saleswoman.

Bring them in, and they will smoke your company. They will enable your company to be highly successful and profitable. The best way to do it is find top people until your company is so large that you have to start to recruit people from scratch and train them from the beginning—but never take your eye off the ball of sales. You need super salespeople because your competitors have super salespeople. The best companies have the best salespeople. Second-best companies have the second-best salespeople. Third-best companies are on their way toward bankruptcy.

The sixth question is *how much will you charge for the product?* You must be very careful about this. It's like shooting at a bull's-eye: if you're off just a small distance, you hit nothing. You'll have no sales at all. Therefore, you have to be really clear about how much you're going to charge—the exact amount that is the very best amount for this market.

One thing I found is this: it's very simple. You have a $10 product. If you change the price to $9.97—that's three cents, just that number, $9.97, versus $10—you'll increase your sales 40 percent, just because of the way that you charge.

The smartest thing you can do, if you're going to start a business, is to go out and pay anything that is required to get a super salesman or a super saleswoman.

I worked with a friend of mine who is now wealthy and retired. He charged $1,000 a year for a series of customer services, but people said no, no, no, because the entrepreneurs who were their customers didn't have $1,000. Most people don't have the cash.

My friend said, "What can we do?" They changed their whole business system: they started to charge $100 per month. People began paying $100 a month, and the sales went up. They tripled the first month, and they just kept going up and going up. He had ten or twelve people working for him. He now has 120 working for him.

He was struggling, but soon he was a millionaire, just by changing the way he charged. That's something to think about. Remember, the customer is always right. If the customer says, "I can't afford it," and you know the customer does have the money over time but doesn't have it all at once, then you restructure. Many companies actually transform their business by changing how they charge.

The seventh question in a business plan is, *how will the product be produced?* This has to be on paper. Think on paper. How will you produce this? Again, companies transform their business by deciding to produce the product or service in a different way. A company will produce it themselves, or they will outsource the production. Sometimes they transform the business completely by taking it all in-house, which is what Amazon did. When they started off, they had a deal with the publishers: they would make the sale online and transfer the sale to the publishers; the publishers would ship it out, charge, and pay Amazon.

This became too cumbersome, so now Amazon has warehouses that are as big as airplane hangars. They have thousands of people, and they recently announced that they're hiring 50,000 people all over the country. They're hiring huge numbers of people to handle all of the distribution internally, because they found that this is the only way that they can get the products to their customers quickly, guarantee shipping and returns, guarantee payment processes, and so on.

That transformed the business. Amazon was a small business, and there were over 300 companies selling books online when they decided to take it in-house. Today they dominate the entire world.

The eighth question is, *how will the product be delivered?* How do you get the goods out of the woods? How do you get the product into the hands of the customer, and who is going to do it? How will it be tracked? How will it be calculated? These seem like small things, but they are not.

I like to use restaurants as an example. You invite people to the restaurant, they come, they sit down, you give them the order, the cook prepares the order. But they're so mixed up that it takes too long to get the food, and the food is cold, or it's overcooked or undercooked, because they haven't thought about the details.

We discovered something recently. It's called Uber Eats. You can go online, and you can find Uber Eats. They'll give you the restaurants that Uber Eats represents, and you can order the food online and push and click on your Uber account. Immediately you will get a confirmation that you have ordered this food, and you'll be told how many minutes it will be before it's delivered. The food will be delivered from your favorite restaurant, hot, piping, delicious. It'll be there on the minute. And now they've shortened the time. Now all over the country people are buying food from Uber Eats.

The ninth question is, *how will the customer be charged?* Uber Eats is perfect because you have your credit-card information in there. They show up at your front door, here's the food, and they walk away. You order from a restaurant, and twenty-two minutes later, all the food is there in your hands. No signing, no anything. It's just like Uber cars.

Each time somebody does something like this, it motivates other entrepreneurs to do it better, faster, cheaper, easier. The opportunities are tremendous.

The tenth question you ask is, *how will the product be installed?* Once the customer has bought it, how will you get the product to the customer? What's the step-by-step process? If you fall apart at this point, people don't get the product on time, or they get the wrong product, or it takes too long.

Best Buy, which has big stores all over the country, got into serious trouble. Their sales went down and down. They said, "OK, where is the market opportunity here?" They found that the primary time when people who bought electronics, like flat-screen televisions and computers, was on the evenings and weekends. They had all of their techies waiting around during the day, but they were only doing business on the evenings and weekends.

Best Buy made this offer. It was a billion-dollar decision: If you buy something from us, we'll match the prices of online vendors, and we will send out our people to install the product or service during the day. If you have a problem or a difficulty with a product or service, we will send out our techies during the day to fix it.

People said, "Oh, my God," because that's their biggest problem. They don't know how to install this stuff. They're not technical. If they have a problem, they don't know how to resolve it. Best Buy had a good staff and changed their job focus so that during the day, they installed, and during the evenings or afternoons, they would sell at the stores.

Best Buy is now one of the biggest success stories in high-tech. You can do all your research and then go to a Best Buy and order your product. You don't have to think about it again. They will take care of you. About 80 to 90 percent of people have no technical skills, like me. How would I install a flat-screen television? How would I put in a musical system with multichannel speakers? I don't know anything about that. If I buy it online, I get it in a box. What do you do with it from there? How many hours do you have to spend trying to figure out how to get this to work?

Best Buy will match the price and install it for you and maintain it at no extra charge. Wow. They went from heading toward bankruptcy to booming.

The eleventh question in your business plan is, *how will the customer be serviced?* The customer has now bought from you. How are you going to take care of that customer so that they are so happy that they buy again and again, and they tell their friends? Every successful company has thought this through.

I have a whole program called "Customers for Life." Before you even contact a customer or communicate with them for the first time—it's called a *customer touch*—you have a process whereby at the end of the process, this customer is yours for life. They buy from you, they're happy, you constantly give them great service. You get back to them quickly, you sell and resell, and you upsell and cross-sell, and then you get referrals and recommendations from happy customers.

The most successful companies have developed systems whereby as many as 85 percent of their customers come from happy customers. It's all thought through in advance, word-for-word, to get the customer to the point where they become customers for life. They buy from you again and again.

One great example, again, is Apple. People buy an Apple phone, then they buy the next one and the next one, and they tell their friends and their family. Can you imagine? As I said, 90 percent of their customers are so happy they're planning to buy upgrades. It's unbelievable. People are shaking their heads that this company is still so profitable year after year. If 90 percent of your customers are so happy that they're planning to buy another one, that's phenomenal. That means the company will just grow and grow and grow.

"Can you give me a referral?" or "Do you know somebody else who would like my product or service?" is the beginning and end of most referral business. The fact is that most people don't want to sell for you. They don't want to be embarrassed. They don't want to ask their

---

Customer Touch: Before you even contact
a customer or communicate with them for the
first time, you set up a process whereby, at the
end of the process, you have a customer for life.

---

friends to buy from you, so you school them: how do you identify someone in your circle who could really be helped with this product? People like to help their friends, so the company would design a system that would teach their customers how to identify ideal customers in their personal database, how to introduce them, and how to open the door, so that it's not a passive thing. It's a very active process. People are always on the lookout, because they've been schooled to look for people in their social circle who could buy the product. Sales are ten times greater from referrals, but it's not just from saying, "Can I have a referral?" There's a system to it.

The twelfth and final question is *who specifically will do all these jobs?* When you start your business, you, as the entrepreneur, do all the jobs. What you have to do is think on paper. You have to develop a system.

The E-Myth and *The E-Myth Revisited*, two excellent books from Michael Gerber on entrepreneurship, encourage you as the business owner to think in terms of a system that can be duplicated, so that once you have started and built your business and made sales, you can make the system so simple that another person could move to another city and duplicate it. Always think in terms of everything you do as a system, word-for-word. How do you contact your customers? How do you produce the product? How do you manufacture it? How do you charge? How do you pay?

What if you had something go wrong with you? Here's the problem with most entrepreneurs: if they leave the business, the business stops. One great question is, how long could your business continue to function if you weren't there for a week or a month? That is the true measure of the health of an entrepreneurial business: how long could your business function if you, the founder, were not there personally?

As soon as I read that, I began to design my business so that I could be gone for as long as a week, and then two weeks, and then four weeks, and six weeks. I could be in Singapore or India or South America, and my company would continue to thrive. Sometimes the company would be more profitable and make more sales when I was gone.

So how do you systematize everything so that someone else can do it? It's like a franchise model.

This is what a business plan is. You think it through, and you ask these questions.

By the way, never dismiss a successful competitor. Always admire your successful competitors. Look up to them, call them up. If you see they're doing well, call them and talk to them and say, "I'm in this business as well, and I see that you guys are doing great. Do you have any advice? How did you manage to make this transition? Or where do you get the people?"

It's quite amazing. Many competitors recognize that you're not their competitor. You're in San Francisco and they're in St. Louis, and they don't care. You call them up and tell them that you really admire their success, and you ask if they could give you some advice. "We keep having this problem," and it's astonishing. They'll say, "We had that problem at the beginning too, and we wrestled with it, and then finally we come up with a solution. Ta-da. The solution will just blow your mind. It'll make you rich."

Always admire. Never denigrate or criticize a successful competitor. Your successful competitors will make you rich. Duplicate them and do them one better. Just one small improvement is all that it takes.

The business plan becomes the foundation, and you continually revisit the foundation. The only question you ask is, does it work? Is it working? Is it generating sales and profitability as I anticipated?

If not, you must go back to the drawing boards. A business plan that is drawn up on a Friday may have to be revised on a Monday because of competitive responses. Your competitors will always act to neutralize any advantage or benefit that you have.

The other thing that I teach in business planning is, first of all, market analysis. Who is your competition in this market? Why should a customer buy from you rather than from someone else? You have to answer that, because

---

"Never denigrate or criticize a successful competitor. Your successful competitors will make you rich. Duplicate them and do them one better. Just one small improvement is all that it takes."
—Brian Tracy

this is what determines if the customer buys from you. Who's your competition, and why should somebody buy from you rather than from your competition?

Another question: you flip it over, and you say, why do people prefer my competition to me? What is it that they offer that, in the customer's mind, makes their product more attractive, and how can I neutralize that attractiveness? How can I do something that's faster, better, cheaper?

It's kind of a national marketing joke. Domino's Pizza: "We're sure fast, but our food sucks. But not anymore." They put it on television. They're making a joke of the fact that Domino's food was not great, but now it's going to be fast *and* great. Their business is booming.

What is the unique added value that you can give your customers that no one else can offer? Unique added value is the number-one reason people buy from you. It is the primary reason you are successful or not. You offer something to your customer that makes your product superior to anything else that's available.

As soon as you develop a unique value-add, your competitors are going to attempt to neutralize it. It's like playing leapfrog as a child. You jump over one child, and they jump over you, and you jump over them. That's what happens in business. You come up with a competitive advantage that causes people to buy from you. Your competitors, who are also very aggressive and want to be successful and make a lot of money, look for a way to jump over you. Then you jump over them. Then they jump over you. This never stops, because the customer always has to be convinced that what you are offering is superior in some way to your competitor's. It can be speed, it can be variety, it can be quality, it can be many different things, but that's why people buy from you.

One of my favorite stories, which summarizes it all, says that on the Serengeti plains of Africa, each morning a lion awakes, and the lion knows that it must run faster than the slowest antelope if it wants to eat that day. Each morning, on the Serengeti plains, an antelope awakes, and the antelope knows it must run faster than the slowest lion if it wants to survive that day.

The moral of the story in entrepreneurship is whether you are a lion or an antelope, when the sun comes up, you'd better be running.

7

Essential #5
Hiring Top Talent and Managing for Success

When I started my entrepreneurial coaching program, I found that entrepreneurs are held back because they do too many little things. They get so bogged down in little things that by the time the day is over, they have not done the important things, and they haven't made sales.

So I put together a structure. It began with the question, why do you hire people to help you? The rule is that 95 percent of your success is going to be determined by the people that you hire to do the critical jobs. That's why Hiring Top Talent and Managing for Success is an absolutely essential subject for every entrepreneur to master.

When I started off, what I found was that you're impatient. You have to get results. You have to make sales. You have to generate revenues, so you hire people quickly. Then they don't work out, and sometimes you have a nightmare.

Earlier I emphasized the importance of being very careful in your hiring and having a labor lawyer, because you can hire a person on Monday, fire them on Tuesday, and end up having to pay them two years' salary.

To attract and keep good people, we say that all work is done by teams. It's one person working with another person—a team can be two people. A team can be you and a part-time person. The manager's work, the business owner's work, is the work of the team. It's what everybody does together that determines your success or failure. Success requires excellent performance by each team member in each key job.

When we brought our entrepreneurs into our program, we would begin by saying, "Hire an assistant, and hire people to do jobs that can be done at a lower average wage than you anticipate earning."

How much do you earn per hour today? This is one of the most important principles that I've taught over the years. What is your hourly income? Simply take your annual income and divide it by 2,000, which is the number of hours that you work in a year. Very simple: just go to your income-tax returns.

Let's say you earn $100,000 a year; that, divided by 2,000, means that you earn $50 an hour. The rule now—which is life-changing—is hire, outsource, downsize, delegate every single task that somebody else can do who works at a lower rate than that. Don't do $10-an-hour work. Don't make photocopies. Don't make pots of coffee. Don't do things that you can hire somebody else to do at a lower rate.

You may say, "I can't afford to hire an assistant," but remember, if you are not doing the work that only you can do and that really pays well, you're going to have to do work that has low value or no value. Entrepreneurs who hire an assistant to take care of the little stuff see their income go up by 50 percent and 100 percent almost immediately, because they are not doing anything of low value. They're only doing the things that matter.

There are only three things that you do as a business owner or an entrepreneur that account for most of your income. If you make a list of everything you do in the course of a week or a month, it'll be twenty, thirty, sometimes forty things, but of those, only three items, three activities, account for 90 percent of the value that you contribute, 90 percent of your income, 90 percent of your financial success.

Ask yourself, "What are my big three?" We call this the Law of Three. If you could only do one thing all day long, which one would contribute the most value to your business and to your income? Write it down, and think about it. Most people have never done this.

Then ask, if you could only do two things all day long, what would be the second activity that would contribute the most value? Then you say, if you could only do *three* things all day long, what would be the third activity that would contribute the most value?

Brian Tracy's *Law of Three*:
If you could only do *three* things all day long,
what would be the three activities that would
contribute the most value? These are the activities
that you should spend most of your time on.

These are the activities that you should spend most of your time on. Do fewer things, but do more important things, and do them more of the time and get better at each one. Then your job is to find someone else to do the other tasks. This is the skill of a manager or an executive, because if you don't find someone else, you'll end up doing it yourself.

That's why some entrepreneurs work ten, twelve, fifteen hours a day, seven days a week, and they accomplish very little. They're exhausted. They're stressed out. It affects their family and everything else, but some of the stuff they're doing is of such low value that it's a waste of their time. But if you don't hire someone else to do it, you're going to end up doing it yourself.

That's the starting point of the question of whom you hire. You hire anybody who can do anything at a lower hourly rate than you. You refuse to do it. You don't use your creativity to work longer, harder hours. You don't come in earlier and work later and work on weekends and evenings. You say, "Whom else can I get to do this?"

Fortunately, today you can hire people to do thirty-minute tasks, one-hour tasks, two-hour tasks. You don't need to do it yourself. You need to use your genius to find someone else to do it so you can do the big three. Delegate everything that anyone else can do at a lower hourly rate than you earn, and free up every minute possible for doing those things that only you can do. Do what you do best, and delegate or discontinue the rest. What do you do best?

Who are great people for your business? When I started off, I would hire people without even thinking about them. They would come in and say, "I want this job, and I can do a great job." They always tell you they can do a great job. You hire them, and you find that they can't even do a good job: they have no experience, or anything else.

The rule is, hire slowly. The most important thing you can do to get good people is to hire them carefully and slowly, just like IBM. They take two years to hire a person, but they expect that person to be with the company for thirty years, and they're willing to take a long time to hire and a long time to train. Small businesses cannot do that. So the most important thing in hiring another person is what I call *transferability of results*. That means that the person that you hire is a person who has gotten the essential results you need them to get in a previous position with another company, and they've done it well.

Big companies can hire people and spend weeks or months to train them from scratch, but small companies, entrepreneurs, have to hire people who can hit the ground running, people who are already good at what they do and can start working the first day.

Some years ago, when my company was growing rapidly, I needed an accountant to run my business. I had many activities going on, and you have to keep accurate track. One of the biggest reasons for small-business failure is loss of control of the accounting department. So I needed an accountant.

I hired someone at random. She turned out to be dreadful. I replaced her with someone else, who was dreadful as well. I'm not an accountant. I'm a sales guy. I'm an entrepreneur. I'm a get-results person. So I just kept hiring people, because I didn't know what I was doing.

I called my accountant and said, "I need to hire a full-time controller."

"OK," she said. "I will interview several people for you, and I will send you three candidates, and you can choose from the three if you like one of them."

She did. She sent me three candidates. The third candidate was a woman named Helen, and she was about fifty-five or sixty years old—a very nice woman, not glitzy or anything, but she was an accountant, a small-business accountant.

I hired her. It came down to negotiating salary. I said, "What kind of salary do you want?" She said "I want $3,000 a month." This was back in the eighties, so it was a good salary. You'd make probably $6,000 today. I said, "I was only planning to pay $2,000." She said, "That's not enough for me. I have expenses."

I said, "I'll make you a compromise. I'll pay $2,500 a month, which is not unreasonable for a competent person. Then after ninety days, we will review your salary, and if everything is working out well, you're happy, I'm happy, we'll raise it to $3,000."

She said, "OK." She was a little bit reluctant. This was Friday or maybe even Saturday; I was interviewing on the weekend. I hired her, and she started on Monday. She came in, she took over all the books, the accounting, the stuff that had been messed up by other people. She came to me and asked me this, came to me and suggested that, came to me and did that.

I was amazed. I had never had such a competent person. I came to her on Monday afternoon and said, "I know we agreed that we would revisit this in ninety days. But I'm raising your salary to $3,000 now," and I did. Then every year, around salary-increase time, I would go to her and say, "You're doing such a good job, I don't want to lose you. I really value you. I'd like to increase your salary. Would that be OK?" She always said yes. We always laughed about that. She worked for me for ten years, and then she retired. She was a wonderful woman.

The point is: hire the people that you need, and hire good people, because then I never had to worry about money, financing, and accounting. Up to that time, the accounting system was out of control. Bankers were threatening to close on my loans, put me out of business. They wanted to seize my house. We had the money in the bank, but the accounts were so messed up that we couldn't even find it.

So find someone who's really, really good, and never cheap out on hiring good people, because, as I've said before, they'll always pay you back far, far more than you pay them.

Never "cheap out" on hiring good people, because they'll always pay you back far, far more than you pay them.

What to Look for in Employees

1. They are excellent at their work.
2. They accept high levels of responsibility.
3. They have a positive mental attitude.

Here are the things that you look for. Number one, *they are excellent at their work*. They do their job well *now*. They are not people that will learn in a week or a month or a year or so on. You're a small business, you're an entrepreneur, and you have to hire people who are already good at what you want them to do.

Number two, *they accept high levels of responsibility*. They're not looking for an entitlement. They're not looking for an easy job.

I've had people apply to me wanting to know if I'm going to provide them with a car and vacations and bonuses and offices. I've said, "You have to understand this is a small business. We don't have the luxury of doing those things. I don't have that stuff. I have to buy my own darn car."

Good employees are not quibbling over this and that. They accept levels of responsibility, and they want to get started. They want to do the work.

Number three, *good employees have a positive mental attitude*. Only hire people that you like. That's not the main condition, and it's not the only condition, but it is a key condition. If you're going to work with that person, you're probably going to spend more time with that employee than you do with your spouse or your children.

Therefore, be really certain that you like this person. If for any reason you don't like the person, even if they appear to be competent, don't hire them. You want people to be happy. You want to create a work environment.

Once, when there was a lot of bickering going on, I brought my staff together and said, "Look, my job is to make sure that everybody here is happy and that we all work together in harmony. So if anybody here is not happy for any reason, then I encourage you to leave. Just go. There's no resentment or anything else. We'll pay you off, but I'm not going to have anybody working here who is not happy and who does not contribute to a harmonious environment."

We had about twenty-two people at that time. We had a couple that were pains in the you-know-where. They were always complaining and gossiping and quibbling and criticizing me or other people. I said, "If you continue to do this, you'll have to go, because it's not helpful to my business. It's taking up too much time and energy." They said, "OK." They sulked a bit, and then they started up complaining and criticizing again.

I fired them both. Everyone in the company was shocked, but they were happy, because they knew I would not allow negative people to be making the work environment an unpleasant place to be. From then on, it was very simple.

I'll show you how to hire people in just a couple of seconds. You only want people who get along well with other people; other people are happy with them. The way you can tell if you have good people is if they laugh a lot. The most important thing for high performance is a positive work environment, where people like their coworkers, they like their work, and they talk. They go out for coffee and lunch, and they socialize.

We've had people who came and worked for me for years and went on to something else. Twenty years later, they still have lunch and dinner and Christmas together. They're still happy together. That's what you're looking for.

Also, use your employees' time well. You are the ultimate disciplinarian. You say, "We work all the time here. We don't play. This is not a place where we sit around and chat and tell jokes and so on." Here's the rule: if they're spending more than 10 percent of their time socializing in a work environment, it means the work is badly organized. It means that people are not clear about what you want them to do, so they do nothing.

Your job as the manager is to make sure that everybody is working, that everybody is busy. You may have too many people. One way to increase efficiency is decrease the number of people working for you. In this recession that we had starting ten years ago, it's quite astonishing how many companies, right up to Fortune 500 companies,

---

If your employees are spending more than 10 percent of their time socializing in a work environment, that means that their work is badly organized; they are not clear about what you want them to do.

---

laid off hundreds and even thousands of people. They've increased their efficiency, increased their productivity, increased their output, because there are fewer people to do the work. They don't have time to waste, and they get along well with others.

Your ability to find and hire the right people is the key to leveraging and multiplying yourself. Sometimes one really productive entrepreneur, if they have a good support staff, can produce ten times as much as a single person without a support staff. That's your job: to multiple and leverage yourself so that you have people producing vastly more than they cost—free plus a profit.

Selection is 95 percent of the success in hiring. It's the most important process. I told you I worked with IBM and Hewlett-Packard and a thousand of the biggest companies in the world. These companies are big because they are very careful about the hiring process. They interview and interview and interview.

The average large company interviews seven times before they hire someone. Some companies will interview ten times, twelve times. I was reading about one company in New York that interviews twenty times. They have a checklist—first interview, second interview, whom the interview is with, and so on. Even down to the receptionist level, they interview twenty-five times. They also have a turnover rate that's less than 1 percent in five years. Once they hire a person, that person stays there for life.

The most successful companies are those that have low turnover. It takes a lot of time and money to hire a person, and then to train and familiarize that person with your business and with your products, services, customers, and other employees. If they don't work out, you lose all of that. You have to hire somebody new.

One reason I have a good company is that I continually pay my people more. I pay them in recognition of the fact that they have skills and abilities and knowledge.

There are three critical skill areas for an employee. First, the skill of doing their job. The second is the skill of knowing all the people outside the company, all the people that influence the company, the customers, the suppliers, the people that you depend on. The third skill area is knowledge of the people inside the company—knowing who reports to whom, and works with whom, who has strengths and weaknesses, who does what, and what's the pecking order and area of responsibility. These things are invisible. They're called intellectual capital, but they're invisible forms of intellectual capital, and a person has to have them to do a good job.

If a person leaves because somebody offers them $100 a month more, you can lose weeks, months, even years of intellectual capital. Now you have to find a new person and create that capital. It's really important to understand that it's not just the person doing the job. It's all the little things they know about how your company functions. It makes them invaluable. It enables them to get results far faster, far better, far more easily than a person who's brand-new.

This also is something to remember: never hire as a solution to a problem. Many people say, "Geez, we have too much to do. Hire someone." During the dot-com boom, companies were hiring several hundred people a week.

Can you imagine? Hiring one person in a small business is a real challenge, but hiring several hundred people—I mean, hiring people by the roomful, because the companies were growing so rapidly. Of course, all those companies collapsed. All those companies disappeared.

Even if you have a problem, even if you have to get the job done, even if you're behind schedule, it's much easier to go slow and hire carefully, take your time, and get the right person the first time rather than doing it quickly.

Poor hiring is very expensive. It costs between three to six times a person's annual income to hire that person and lose them, because it takes so much time to train them and to work with them, to supervise them. And these are invisible costs. Sometimes you have to pay for outside hiring firms.

Some people say it takes as much as ten times a person's salary to hire a person and keep them. You're paying them $30,000 a year. It may be costing you $300,000 in invisible costs. Here's what they found. Business consultant Dan Kennedy said all these costs are invisible, and the companies that have the lowest turnover have the highest profits in every industry.

That's why companies that are really big and powerful are very careful about hiring, and as a result, people produce far more. There are far fewer mistakes, far fewer losses, far fewer difficulties.

If you have low turnover, you have high profits. All costs of high turnover are invisible costs. Companies can go broke if they have a high level of turnover, and they won't know where the money went.

I keep saying over and over again that your ability to think is the most important skill you have, so in hiring, you think through the jobs. I call this the *iron triangle*. Iron triangle point number one is, *what are the results expected of the person?* What do you actually want them to achieve by the end of the day?

The Iron Triangle of Hiring

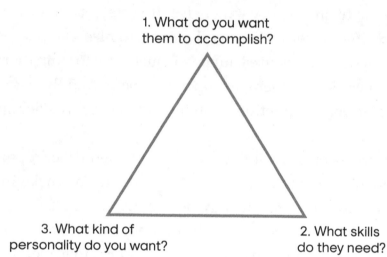

1. What do you want them to accomplish?

3. What kind of personality do you want?

2. What skills do they need?

If you're hiring a salesperson, it's really easy. You want them to achieve a certain level of sales each day, each week, each month. For other people, you have to stand back and say, what do I want them to accomplish?

I write a lot—book after book after book. One of my secretary's jobs was to type up the manuscripts, so I developed a method of dictation, writing, layout, and so on. We worked together, and she beautifully typed book after book after book, and it made an extraordinary difference to me. Shirley worked with me for twelve years. She did fabulous work, and I paid her really well because she was free plus a profit. She enabled me to produce so much high-quality work.

So think: what results are expected? Usually in a job several results are expected. Make a list: what are the three big ones, the three biggest and most important things that you need that person to do?

Whether they can do a lot of little things may be important, or it may not be. But there are probably three things—the big three—that, if they do them, and they do them well, and consistently, will make an enormous contribution for you.

The second part of the triangle is the *skills required*. What skills will a person require in order to do those three main jobs or to get those major results? This is a matter of past experience. When you're interviewing a person, always ask them about what they've done in the past, whom they've done it for, and what results they've gotten. Remember, you're looking for a person who has already gotten the results you want and has done it really well.

The third part of the triangle is *the personality attributes that are necessary*. What kind of a person do you want to hire? Friendly, warm, helpful, cooperative, and so on. Large companies have found that the major reason people are fired is not that they are not great in a technical area. It's because they just don't get along well with others.

This goes all the way up to Fortune 500 CEO levels. Just look at the famous story about the founder of Uber. Obviously brilliant, built a $70 billion company in five years, and the board of directors asked him to step down because he is a jerk. Steve Jobs couldn't be fired, because he owned the company, but he was a jerk as well. He was very difficult and insulting. The head of Xerox a few years ago was fired because he was a jerk. He would insult and shout at and swear at people.

Personality is really important. Hire nice people. Hire only nice people. Even if that person is a genius, if they're not a pleasant person to work with, pass them by.

The next step is to write out the job description. Imagine that there is a perfect-person factory. If you send this factory an order, they will send you the perfect person for this job. Think on paper. Force yourself to think on paper and write it down. The most amazing thing is that this activates the Law of Attraction in the universe and will help to attract the perfect person into your life.

I'll give you an example. I started a new business on executive training, using video, workbooks, and training people to go into companies. I needed a vice-president to run that whole division. I didn't have someone, and one of the rules is, if you do not have a champion to spearhead a new product or service, don't launch it, because it'll never be successful.

I sat down, and I followed my own advice. I wrote down a list of thirty-four things that I was looking for in the perfect person. This is a highly paid position. We're talking about $75,000 base and $150,000 possible income. I wanted all these things—experience in my business and knowledge of the business and sales, a nonsmoker, and physically fit.

The *Perfect Person Factory* Exercise:
Think on paper. Write out a job description, and in
addition, write down the qualities of the ideal candidate
for the job. Imagine if you send this written document
to a factory like an order, they will send you the perfect
person for the job. This will activate the *law of attraction*.

Then I had a man call me up out of the clear blue sky; I'd never seen or heard of him before. He said, "I work for one of your promoters, selling your seminars from office to office in distant cities. I've just finished a job, and I was thinking about you. I was thinking there might be an opportunity for me to work for you, so I would like to come and talk to you for a few minutes, if I could."

He was a nice guy, intelligent, and he'd worked for me indirectly in the past, so I brought him in. I said, "I can give you thirty minutes, because I'm really busy." He came in, I met him, and I spent three hours with him. The guy was excellent. He had all the right qualities, personality, everything, and I hired him and put him to work.

He worked with me for almost a year. Not only did he have all thirty-four qualities—I went over the list with him about a month later—but he had more. He had the ability to design computer programs for marketing and sales. The guy was a genius. He was a lifelong student and was constantly upgrading his skills. His name was Carl. I still remember him today.

So one of the most important things you can do is think on paper. Make out a list and then imagine you're going to send an order to this perfect-person factory. Write it out exactly as if it's an order: I'm searching for a person with these qualities, attributes, abilities, skills, personality. Then you mail it off. Your likelihood of getting the perfect person will be phenomenal.

Once you have that perfect description, tell your friends or coworkers, "I'm looking for a person like this. What do you think?" They'll say, "Maybe you want to have more of this or less of that. Did you remember to put in this and that?"

Get a consensus on the person you're looking for. Tell everybody in your company you're looking for a person like this. Very often they will know someone in their family, friends, background, or history that's the perfect person.

Many companies hire a minimum of 90 percent of their people by internal recommendation. They do it by writing up a very clear description and discussing it with their staff and teams. Small companies can do this quite quickly. Then everybody goes away with a written description, and then they ask their spouses, "What do you think about this? Do you know anybody like this?"

"Well, my friend so-and-so, whom I went to school with, just moved back into town here a month ago and is still between jobs." Sometimes they'll bring you the perfect person.

Go slowly. Force yourself to slow down, and the way you slow down is write it out. If you don't write it out, your chances of making a hiring mistake can be enormous. A hiring mistake can be very expensive and cost you far more in time and aggravation than if you just slow down.

Finally, cast a wide net. Tell others. Tell lots of other people that you're looking for this person. The more people who know that you're looking for a person, the more likely it is somebody will know.

I have a couple of friends who do this. When they're expanding their business, they'll call me up, and they'll say, "I'm looking for a person like this. Do you know anybody in your circle of friends? I'll send you over a written description." Once a year I'll get something like that. I always say to myself, that's so intelligent, so smart. Instead of guessing or running ads or hiring personnel agencies, just put out the word. People will say, "Ah yes, I just spoke to someone who maybe knows someone who's talking about someone."

Now the interviewing process. Again, I've gotten this from working with some of the biggest companies in the world. They have spent fortunes and decades developing interviewing processes. There are certain simple things that you do that make an extraordinary difference.

Number one, look for *achievement history*. What has the person done in the past? Remember, transferability of results. The reason you hire someone is they've already done what you need them to do. Many companies today are finding that if they can find someone who has a track record of success in this new endeavor at some other company, the other company's already paid to teach them how to do this. That can save weeks and months and enormous amounts of money in getting to the same level of performance.

In your interview, focus on what they've done in the past and whom they've done it for and what their results were. More than 50 percent of answers to these questions turn out to be false or exaggerated.

Next, look for *a sense of urgency*. A really good person wants the job, and they want to start now. As a test question, I say, "If we were to reach an agreement, and this is the right job for you, and you're the right person for this job, how soon would you be willing to start?" The right person wants to start now. They want to start immediately.

I had a secretary, Judy, a wonderful woman. I needed a personal assistant, and the personal assistant does a lot of the work in my business. She was sent to me by someone else, and I interviewed her. I asked her this question. She said, "I really want this job. I think I could do a great job here. I have to give two weeks' notice at my current job, but I would be willing to work evenings and weekends for free to learn this job so that as soon as I get free from where I am, I can start immediately."

I hired her right there, and she started coming in at 5:15. She'd go to work and start organizing things. In less than two weeks, she came in full-time, and she was just as good for the rest of the time she was with me as at the beginning. The only reason she left four years later was that she'd had two children, and she had a third. She just didn't have the time. But she's still a friend of almost everybody in our office. They have lunch together, they talk together, they chat together.

Most of the people who work for me have this kind of relationship. They're all friends with one another because they know they're always welcome in the company. They can come in any time, meet with us, see people, and so on.

In addition, look for *intelligent questions*. A study by *Fortune* magazine found that 72 percent of the likely success of a person will be determined by the questions they ask during the interview. If a person sits there and responds passively or doesn't ask questions, it means that they're afraid of saying the wrong thing, but a really good staff person will interview *you*.

I did a one-day seminar called "How to Get the Job You Want." It's very popular. Thousands of people listened to that program and went out and got a new job or a better job. One of the things I taught was informational interviewing.

In informational interviewing, you interview the boss rather than the boss interviewing you. You ask a lot of questions. You have your questions prepared. You have a list of questions about the company: its background and past and the product and service and the customers and the market and the strengths and weaknesses of the business. You ask a lot of questions, because this is your life.

From the employer's point of view, you're asking a person to come and donate part of their life for an indefinite period of time to this job. They want to know what their probabilities of future advancement are, how much they can expect to earn in the future, what job will they

---

Look for the following qualities in each interviewee:
- Strong achievement history
- A sense of urgency
- A person who asks intelligent questions.

---

be doing in a year, two years, and so on. The more questions they ask, the more likely they are to be excellent employees.

Then there's the Rule of Three. The Rule of Three is one of the most important things I ever learned. I've taught it to company executives in some of the biggest companies in the country, and they make it a rule: every single person who has hiring authority must learn and practice the Rule of Three.

The Rule of Three for Hiring

1. Interview at least *three* people.
2. Interview the person you like the most at least *three* times.
3. Interview the person you like in at least *three* different places.
4. Have at least *three* other people interview the candidate.

The Rule of Three says that you interview at least three people for a job. You never hire after you've interviewed one person. I was involved in a business about five years ago, and the manager was a sales guy but a terrible manager. He decided that he wanted to free himself from the day-to-day work, which was his job. I'd invested a lot in this company, and it wasn't doing well.

So he just up and decided that he was going to hire somebody to do all this stuff that he was supposed to be doing but was doing poorly. He was loading groceries into his car in a supermarket parking lot, and he started talking to the guy in the next car, who was loading groceries as well. They had a little chat, and my manager said to the guy, "Where are you working at right now?"

"I'm between jobs," he said.

"How would you like to become president of my company?"

The manager hired this guy as the president of the company and brought him in. The two of them together, arm in arm, bankrupted the company in six months.

Think of that. How on earth can you hire somebody in a potentially multimillion-dollar business because you met him putting groceries in your car in a parking lot? No interview, no background check. He paid him far too much money, and the guy knew nothing about the job. I always think about that as a great example.

So you interview at least three people, and then you take the person that you like the most. Some companies will interview five or ten or twenty people. With the person you like the most, you interview them at least three times. Even if the person looks fantastic in the first meeting, meet with them again. The person who looks great the first time looks average the next time, and very often looks dreadful the third time, so delay. Go slowly. Slow down the process. Put your foot on the brakes. Don't hire quickly. Hire slowly.

Next, interview the person that you like in three different places. Human beings have what I call the *chameleon effect*. They actually change their behavior and their personalities when you move them around.

Hewlett-Packard has a seven-interview system. It's a minimum of seven interviews, with a minimum of four managers. A person comes in to be interviewed, and if the first interviewer likes them, they pass them on to the second interviewer, third interviewer, and the fourth.

Then they have a joint interview, in which they will have two of the managers interview, and then three, four, five managers interview. They slow down the process.

Next, they invite the candidate and his or her wife or husband out to a nice restaurant for dinner. By this time, the candidate is thinking, "I'm going to get the job. This is great, and this is the final formality. We go out for dinner." So they go out for dinner to a nice restaurant, and the manager brings his wife or husband, and they just chat and so on. They think this is the final wrap-up: social conversation. However, it's an interview, and the interview is very subtle. It's to find out how this couple works together. How do they talk? Are they friendly? Are they polite? Problems at home? How do they treat the waiter? How do they treat the serving staff? Do they treat them with graciousness? Are they polite and friendly? Because they're going to be dealing with the company's customers. How do they deal with the spouse of the interviewer? Do they treat this person like an equal, or do they see them as a second-hand person just brought along on a date? The way that the prospect behaves at the seventh interview determines whether they get hired at all.

Many companies have different tricks and techniques like this. Have at least three other people interview the person. Don't ever make a hiring decision by yourself again for the rest of your life.

The biggest mistakes I made in my early career as an entrepreneur is that I would meet a person and hire them in one meeting. I've hired people on a Monday and fired them on a Tuesday because on Monday they seemed to be really impressive; by Tuesday they'd revealed their true selves. Then I started to interview multiple times so that I could see how they were going to behave the first time, the second time, the third time.

In my company, for years and years I would have at least three people interview the candidate. I'd say, "I really enjoyed talking to you, and we want to make sure we make a good decision here, so you should know as much as possible about the company and the people. I'm going to introduce you to so-and-so, and you can ask him any questions that you want about the business and how it works."

The employee had been primed and knew that I would be bringing the candidate in for an interview. They would chat casually, not boss to candidate, but peer to peer. They'd talk about the business and life and family and what they'd done in the past.

Then this employee would tell the candidate, "Let me introduce you to someone else that you should talk to as well." It'd be a minimum of three people. Today in my company, there is a minimum of seven. When they're looking at a new person, this person speaks to a minimum of seven people around the place. They talk and take them out to lunch before making a hiring decision.

One example locked this in for me. I interviewed this woman. She was friendly. She was charming. She was witty. She was experienced. Seemed like the perfect hire. I was brimming because I was really happy to be hiring this good person. I took her next door to interview with another man and another person and another. Afterwards I said, "What do you think?"

"Absolutely not. This woman is a disaster. First of all, she just got out of jail for embezzlement. This is an accounting position. She is a dope addict, a recovering dope addict."

I was hiring a nightmare, but when she was talking to me, she was very impressive and friendly and warm and helpful. When she was talking to a peer, a person at her level, it all came out.

So I followed their advice, and I never hired anybody that my staff did not approve of again. Now we have almost zero turnover. If a person does turn over, it's because they do not have the ability to develop new skills, or they have to go somewhere else to get married, or something similar. We had two women in our office who were superstars, and they got married. Life moves on.

To sum it up, interview at least three people. Interview the person you like at least three times. Interview in at least three places, and then have three other people interview them and give you their opinion. If you're starting off as an entrepreneur and you don't have staff, then have the person interviewed by a friend of yours. You agree to interview your friend's candidates as well; one hand washes the other. This will save you a lot of time and aggravation.

Another requirement is check résumé references personally. The person who hires must do the résumé checking. That means calling the person that the candidate worked for before. Because of our litigious society, nobody's going to say anything that's going to get them into trouble; you understand that. So you say, "I am looking at hiring this person to do this job. May I ask you a couple of questions about him or her?"

They'll say, "OK, sure." They're very cautious, because they don't want to get into a problem.

Ask, "Can you tell me if you think he or she would be appropriate for this particular job? The output responsibilities would be this, the results we want them to get would be that."

They'll say yes or no. They'll give you a little information.

You'll ask, "Would you have any advice or recommendations for me in hiring this person?" I remember one case when they said, "Just one little thing: she has a big-company mentality. A very nice person, but she has a big-company mentality." It seemed pretty innocuous, so I just said, "Thank you."

He meant that she was a disaster. She had worked for a large company, and she was in HR, and she was used to assigning all work to other people. When she came to work for me, her job was to interact with our consultants and trainers around the country.

The first thing she did was shut off her telephone and refuse to take phone calls from anyone. We'd announced to everybody that she was going to be their personal support person, yet she wouldn't take any calls. She would have everything put on hold, and she found an assistant in the office and said, "You call these people back."

After a week or two I found out. Customers were calling me, saying, "We can never hear anything back from her. We can't get any answers to any questions." I confronted her, and she said, "No, no. You don't understand. That's not my job. I'm the senior HR advisor, and if they have any questions or problems, they can write or leave a message, and I'll have this other woman, Susan, get back to them."

We're a little company. Everything is one-on-one, face-to-face. In a small company, there are no degrees of separation. If a person has a question or a problem or a need, they need a solution immediately. They want to make a sale, they want to get closure, they want to get a check. She danced around working for about two or three months. I finally fired her. She didn't work for two or three years. Nobody would hire her. They checked on her better than I did, and she would never give me as a reference.

Another question you ask is, "Would you hire this person again?" If the person says no, you say, "Could you tell me why not?" Very often you'll get a precious piece of information.

That, by the way, is the acid test. If a previous employer would not hire them back again, you would be a fool to hire them. They're telling you, "Red alert, red alert," but they're not exposing themselves to any liability. If you say, "I would not hire this person," you don't have to give a reason. That should tell you.

I was talking to a manager about a candidate for personal assistant. I asked, "Would you hire this person back again?" and he said, "Absolutely. She's the best person I ever had in this job. The only reason I had to let her go is that the company changed, and we went out of this business, we went into that business, and her job disappeared, but I would hire her back in a minute." Whoa. So I hired her. She worked for me for three years. She did a great job.

The last question I ask just before I go is, "Is there anything else I should know?" This is the time the dam will break. They will very often say, "Well, she likes her marijuana or dope, or she sure likes her whiskey" or something. They will throw something out there that is a red alert.

So go through the checking of résumés and references personally and make notes. Write it down, write it down, write it down. You may speak to two or three or four different people. Don't trust to your memory to remember who said what about whom.

The next rule is, hire slow and fire fast. This is what the biggest companies have learned: go very slowly, but if you make a mistake, fire them quickly. There's a basic rule that says that the best time to fire a person is the first time it crosses your mind. If you think you've made a mistake, you've made a mistake. Cut it off. Cut your losses quickly.

Finally, start them off right, and start them off strong. When you start a person on a new job, load them with work. Give them ten things to do, and the next day give them ten things more. The big mistake that many companies make is to allow people to settle in—come to work, meet their coworkers, sit at their desk, and put up their pictures.

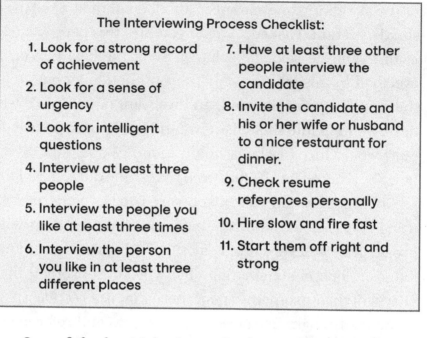

The Interviewing Process Checklist:

1. Look for a strong record of achievement

2. Look for a sense of urgency

3. Look for intelligent questions

4. Interview at least three people

5. Interview the people you like at least three times

6. Interview the person you like in at least three different places

7. Have at least three other people interview the candidate

8. Invite the candidate and his or her wife or husband to a nice restaurant for dinner.

9. Check resume references personally

10. Hire slow and fire fast

11. Start them off right and strong

One of the best jobs I ever had was when I'd just finished my university exams for my MBA in my thirties. I got home from the interview at 3:30, and the phone rang. It was the big boss, and he asked, "Have you thought about coming to work for me?" I said, "Yes, I'd like to do it." He said, "Great. Let's get started."

This was Friday afternoon at 3:30. I said, "I'll come in Monday morning. What time would you like me to be there?"

He said, "What about now?"

His office was about twenty minutes away from my apartment. "OK," I said. "I'll be there in twenty minutes."

He gave me the smallest office in the whole complex and sat me down with a list of jobs. That was my starting point, and we were in that office until 6:00 p.m. I started working on the weekend. By Monday morning, I was drowned. I just drowned in that job for almost two years. I learned more and earned more than I could ever have dreamed possible, because he loaded me with work to do.

So when you hire somebody, load them with work, and then load them with more and more. People complain about having too much work to do, but they love to be overwhelmed with work.

Now let's discuss managing those employees for success. Here it is very simply. Some researchers did one of the most extensive tests on high-performance business profitability and business growth. They looked at tens of thousands of businesses in twenty-two countries. They had 150 researchers, and they worked on this for twelve years to finally say what the keys to high performance are.

There are basically three things that account for 80 or 90 percent of all performance in all jobs. The analysts found that companies that are the most adamant about these three main activities are the companies that are the most successful, profitable, prosperous, and happy.

Rules for High Performance

1. Clear goals and objectives
2. Clear measures and standards
3. Clear deadlines and schedules

Number one is *clear goals and objectives*. As I said before, my favorite word is *clarity*. Ninety-five percent of all problems, difficulties, and goals can be resolved with greater clarity. The problem is lack of clarity: ambiguity. A person's not clear about what they're expected to do. So clarity, clarity, clarity with regard to goals and objectives.

You really can't have much of an effect on a personality style. It's inbred. It's like eye color. However, by being absolutely crystal-clear about what you want and need that person to do, you can dramatically increase their enthusiasm and motivation. People love to be clear about what you want. "Just tell me what you want." You heard that over and over again.

The researchers interviewed tens of thousands of employees and asked them, "Think of the best boss you ever had."

"The best boss I ever had was so-and-so."

"When you look back, what were the characteristics or qualities of this best boss?"

The answer was always, "I always knew exactly what he wanted me to do. I always knew exactly what she wanted me to do. There was never any ambiguity about expectations, so I could come to work, and I could do exactly the work I was supposed to do."

The second quality of the best bosses, according to this study, was consideration. Consideration was, "I felt like my boss cared about me as a person rather than as just a worker." But number one was "I always knew what he or she wanted me to do. I always knew what my goals were." I think this is the biggest of all.

Number two is that the employer is *absolutely clear about measures and standards*, so that each person knew exactly how to measure their work—how you could tell if the job was done well, and how you could tell if it was done better. They sat down, and they became very clear about the goal and about how to measure whether it has been achieved, whether the job has been done in an accurate way. People always had a target to aim at.

The job of the manager is to make the employee feel like a winner. That's the very best standard for the very best companies: everybody in the company feels great about themselves because they feel like winners.

How do you enable people to feel like winners? You enable them to win. How can they win? The answer is that they're clear about what you want them to do and how it can be measured. If they do it to the measure that you set out, it's like crossing a finish line in a race. They feel they've won. If you want high performance, enable people to feel high-performing.

Number three is *clear deadlines and schedules* for the accomplishment of a task. Almost all of your problems with morale, with interactions between managers and staff, come because people do not know clearly what you want them to do. Nor do they know clearly how you're going to measure it. "How can I measure whether I've done a good job?"

People naturally want to do a good job. You have to enable them to do a good job by giving a target to aim at. It's like running a race—I know when I've crossed the finish line. I know when I have won.

Those three things are a very simple way of taking anybody and making them an excellent manager: sitting down with one person or more and discussing and agreeing on what everyone is supposed to do, how it will be measured, and when it needs to be done. Employees know what they're doing, but they also know what everybody else is doing—with complete clarity, feedback, questions, and answers. Shared goals and shared measures are a powerful method of motivation and getting high performance.

When I worked with Hewlett-Packard, this was a central part of the entire business worldwide: they would sit down together, and they would talk and discuss a project, for however long it took, so that everybody knew exactly what the group was supposed to do and what each person in the group was supposed to do and when it was supposed to be done.

They managed by task completion, so the method of management for the leader was, *how's it going*? You don't need long, detailed analyses or performance appraisals. You just need absolute clarity about the job and how it's going. "If you're having trouble achieving the goal for whatever reason, how can I help you? My job is to make it possible for you to do your job."

What I've just explained to you is, I think, the totality of the very best of modern management, and it is easy. You can understand it and apply it immediately. If you want your child to be successful as an adult, you want them to get good grades. If you want them to get good grades, you have to be clear what good grades are and when the assignments are due.

A young person should get into a habit, like breathing in and breathing out, of being clear about what you need to do to be successful. Be clear about how it's measured—grades, standards—and about when it has to be accomplished.

This really covers 80 to 90 percent of success and happiness in the world of work. People are only happy when they feel productive and valuable, when they feel they are making progress and moving forward. When they feel that they are accomplishing something that's moving themselves and their companies forward, they feel happy, and as a result they are naturally motivated and stimulated to do even more of it.

People love to talk about their work and to be clear about their work, how to do it, and how to do it better. So this is a very simple concept. You can use it to become one of the best managers, bosses, entrepreneurs in the world.

If you want to be successful with your customers, find out the big three for the customer. What does the customer really want to achieve in their life, and how will they measure it? How will they know that they've been successful? And when does the customer want it?

Any deviation from those can lead to anger, frustration, demoralization. The job of the manager or company owner is to make sure that everybody has those big three.

Some people wonder if Gen X people and millennials need to be managed differently from previous generations. I have four younger people in my house. They want more independence, they want more freedom, they want to be asked their opinion, they want to be more involved in their work, and they want more opportunities for individuality.

The biggest goal for millennials today is to feel a sense of forward movement, forward progress. How do you instill within young people a sense that they're making progress, that they're becoming better, that they're doing a good job, they're valuable, they're important, they're making a difference in the world?

Again, very clear goals, clear measures, and clear deadlines. Then just stand back and let them go. Then they can express their unique personalities. Many companies today with millennials are just simply saying, "Here's the job, the big three, and if you come in early or you stay later, or you work weekends or evenings or different parts of the day, it's up to you. You're responsible, and the objective, the measure, is separate from you."

In these situations, you can't just say, "I'm doing a good job," because it's clear whether you are or not. It's a question of whether you're fulfilling the big three. You have the ability to express your personality, to work hard, to stay up late at night, to work with your coworkers, and everything else. It's so simple and clean and clear and positive, and it's not based on somebody's personality saying, "You did a good job. You did a poor job." It's really clear.

It's exactly like if you're a salesperson. You can measure how well you're doing by the sales that you bring in.

How do you instill within young people a sense that they're making progress, that they're becoming better, that they're doing a good job, they're valuable, they're important, they're making a difference in the world?

It's not a matter of opinion. It's not a matter of personality. Did you get the results? Did you get them on time? Did you get them to the agreed-upon standard?

This is the key to the future. Why does it work? Someone once said that everything in human life has to be simple, because God only created simple people. The simpler that you can make it, the easier it is for people to perform at their best and to feel really good about themselves.

8

Essential #6
Sales and Marketing:
The Fuel of Your
Business Growth

Let's conclude this book with a topic that is absolutely essential—some consider it to be the lifeblood of any business—sales and marketing. In some respects, all that I've said so far depends on the ability to generate sales with consumers.

You can have the right mindset, a rock-solid business plan, qualified and dependable people, and a solid foundation of financial funding, but all of that will amount to nothing without the ability to generate consistent sales to your targeted consumers.

Some may ask this question: what if there's a person who plans to pursue entrepreneurship, but either has no interest in sales and marketing or doesn't feel that the topic suits their personality? Is it true that every entrepreneur must be a salesperson?

There are many approaches to this question. One of my favorites is from Dan Kennedy: whatever business you are in, you are in the marketing business. You are in the business of attracting people to buying your product or service and paying you money for it. If you do that, you succeed; if you don't do that, you fail, and everything else is secondary.

There's a book written by Michael Porter at Harvard called *Competitive Advantage*. He's considered to be the greatest guru on marketing. The book is almost 600 pages long. I have it. I have not read it all, but it's a great book. Porter is often paid a million dollars a year as a consultant by major corporations to give them insights on how to market better.

Let's start off by stating the difference between *marketing* and *selling*. *Marketing* is attracting people to your offering. Say you own a restaurant. You're with a group of people, and you ask, "Is anybody here hungry? People say, "Oh, I'm hungry." Great.

That's marketing. It's identifying people who are prospective customers for what you sell. *Selling* is when you say, "Now let me tell you why you should come to my restaurant rather than to any other place where you can eat."

Marketing is getting them to raise their hand, getting them to express an interest. Selling is persuading them,

"Whatever business you are in, you are in
the marketing business." —Dan Kennedy

converting them into a customer. They're two separate actions.

Marketing consists of four critical behaviors. We call them the four laws, the four pillars, of marketing strategy. I teach these in all of my business courses. Most, I would say 90 percent, of business owners don't know them. As a result, they are functioning far below their potential: they could be earning ten, twenty times as much.

The Four Pillars of Marketing Strategy

1. Specialization
2. Differentiation
3. Segmentation
4. Concentration

The first is *specialization*. Specialization is the answer to the question, in what area of customer satisfaction do you specialize?

You can specialize in a particular type of customer. A perfect example is Walmart. Walmart specializes in people who live from paycheck to paycheck—the bottom 70 percent of the market. These are people who don't have a lot of money, yet they want to provide for their families. After all, the major driving force for most people is to provide well for their family—clothes, refrigerators, cosmetics, furniture.

Walmart started off with the idea that they would be the dominant provider of products for the average consumer. That's what they do. So they said, "What does that mean?" If you specialize in this customer, you offer almost every product or service that this customer can consume in their family life. Walmart now sell computers and televisions. They basically sell everything that people need, and they guarantee it, because their customers can't make buying mistakes. They can't buy something and throw it in the cupboard and never wear it again if it's not appropriate, as other people can.

Albert Einstein said that you must be able to explain your answers to a six-year-old child. Then you must have the six-year-old turn and clearly explain your answers to another six-year-old and have both understand. If you were a businessperson and a six-year-old asked what area you specialize in, what would be your answer?

Lack of clarity about this question—confusion, ambiguity, specializing in too much, too little, so that the customer does not understand instantly, like a six-year-old—means you have to go back to the drawing boards.

The second type of specialization could be in a technology. Apple specializes in high-tech. They don't manufacture refrigerators or shoes. Google specializes in information. Amazon specializes in products that can be sold online and then delivered through conventional methods. They started with books; now, at my estimation, they have 300 million products. Almost every product in the world is available online, because these are products that can be viewed, specified, ordered, paid for, and shipped out.

Another type of specialization is specialization within a particular market. Some people say, "My market is going to be this town, this city, or this country. My market is going to be worldwide" and so on. What market, or markets, do you want to specialize in? These can overlap. They can double up on each other, but you have to specialize.

People have to know that you specialize in this market. One restaurant specializes in seafood. Another specializes in steak or pasta. The customer has to know with instant clarity that this is the area where you specialize and where you strive to be excellent. This is where you strive to be excellent, which brings you to number two.

The second pillar is called *differentiation*. What do you do that makes your product or service superior to that of your competitors? What makes it so superior that people will choose and often pay more for your product or service?

Michael Porter's *Competitive Advantage,* and other books written about this, all focus on developing an area of differentiation: competitive advantage. They call it your *unique selling proposition*, the one thing that you offer that no other competitor offers but that customers care about.

Unique Selling Proposition: The one thing that you offer that no other competitor offers, but that customers care about.

Some people say, "My product is the best because of this," but it turns out that customers don't care about this feature. This is really important to understand. It has to be something that customers care about.

As I've stressed before, you must have a product that matters in the lives of your customers. It must make a difference in their lives, and it must be superior in some way to any other product that attempts to make that difference. It must move people or connect with people emotionally.

My favorite example is the iPhone. I will say to my audience, "Let me give an example of a product that matters. Have you ever gotten in your car and driven off a few blocks or a few miles, and realized you left your phone at home? What do you do?" Everybody says that they turn around immediately and go back and get the phone. The phone matters to them. This is an important part of their lives.

Not all products can matter. They can't all be so important that people are emotionally connected to them, but you strive for this all the time. Again, using an example of a restaurant: there are lots and lots of restaurants, often within walking distance of lots of other restaurants, so getting food is not what matters.

What really matters is that the restaurant must have a certain level of quality of food. But it's also how customers are treated. The best restaurants and restaurant chains want their guests to feel happy. They want them to feel good about themselves. When you come in, they greet you, they're happy to see you, and they seat you. They thank you for coming, and they give you good service. You sit there, and you beam. It's as we said before about Disney. Disney resort experiences are magic. People who come back from a Disney resort experience are happy. They beam. They brag to one another that they purchased Disney products and Disney services.

Nordstrom department store is famous for customer service. Every person who shops at Nordstrom for any period of time has a Nordstrom story, and it's about something that Nordstrom did for them that was remarkable. They brag about how they had this Nordstrom experience, or how a member of their family had this Nordstrom experience. That's what makes a company a great company. It makes the company the first choice.

When I first moved to San Diego, we asked people, "What's the best department store for your family?" People said, "Nordstrom. You have to go to Nordstrom," so we went to Nordstrom, and we became—they call us Nordies. I'm a Nordy.

I'm a father, a husband, and I have to do Christmas shopping every year. I go to Nordstrom. I know that they will take care of me. I will walk in and go up to a salesclerk in any department. I'll say, "I need to buy gifts for my family, and here are their ages and sexes and interests and so on. Can you help me?"

By the time I walk out of that store, I will have gift-wrapped, age-appropriate, sex-appropriate, and interest-appropriate gifts for every single member of my family, and I can go home and put up the Christmas tree. My family members will all be happy, and if they're not delighted for any reason at all, Nordstrom will take the product back and replace it. If they decide they don't want it a year from now, Nordstrom will take it back, no questions asked, and replace it or refund it.

So I think, "Christmas is coming, but I don't have to worry about it." Typical male—hates to shop. I just go down to Nordstrom, walk in, approach the first clerk, and that clerk will basically put their arms around me, take care of me right until the end of the process, and load the stuff in my car.

That's why I talk about this. Even readers are thinking, "I want to go to Nordstrom." I like that. By the way, the highest level of business is where people bring their friends to buy from you because you make them feel so good.

So you have to have one area of differentiation, one area of excellence, one product or service difference that is important, that matters, that connects with the customer.

As Drucker said, if you don't have competitive advantage, you don't compete, or if you don't have competitive advantage, develop a competitive advantage. A competitive advantage is the absolutely minimum necessary for you to build and grow your company.

If you're thinking of starting a business, remember the six-year-old standing there asking you questions. The six-year-old asks, "What area are you going to specialize in, and what is it that you do better than anybody else in the whole world in this area? What is it that you offer that nobody else has?"

Step number three, the third pillar of marketing strategy, is called *segmentation*. That's where you look at all the different customers in the market, and you realize that

> You have to have one area of differentiation,
> one area of excellence, one product or service
> difference that is important, that matters,
> that connects with the customer.

they are not all your customers. So you have to select the customers who will most benefit from your area of specialization and excellence: the ones who want it more than anyone else, and who are willing to pay more for it. It matters to them. That's why, with a really good product, when you present the benefit or the improvement or change that will take place in the customer's life if they use your product, the customers ask only, "How can I get it? How can I use it? What's the process?" They don't say, "How much is it? It costs too much."

I had rotator-cuff surgery on my shoulder four or five years ago. It was quite serious. There are four sinews, which are like fishing lines or cables, that hold an arm onto a shoulder, and I had hurt one of them. If you've hurt one, you can use physiotherapy and stretching and motion to gradually bring it back.

What I did was foolish. I took painkillers, and I swam, and I continued to use the shoulder. One by one, three of the four cables snapped. When I finally went in to see the doctor, the pain was excruciating. The doctor put me into an MRI and took X-rays and said, "Oh, my Lord. This is a very serious operation, and it's going to require a very serious procedure." We set it up as soon as possible, because I could barely live with the darn thing.

When I got a bill back from him, it was $83,000 for a three-and-a-half-hour surgery. However, I asked, "Am I going to have to wear a great, big cast held up over my head and so on?" He said, "You will be able to walk out of the hospital with your arm by your side," which is phenomenal. I thought it was going to be a multiweek nightmare of healing. He was absolutely correct: "If you follow the instructions for recuperation, you will back to swimming at a mile at a time within twelve months," and I was.

I learned later that this doctor is one of the most respected shoulder surgeons in the world. For three and a half hours, he got $83,000. Interestingly, the next day we got another bill for this surgery for $83,000. The first bill was $83,400, and the second bill was $83,500. We thought there must be a mistake; they must have duplicated the bills.

No. Bill number one was for the surgical activities, three and a half hours. Bill number two was for the hospital and the clinic and the anesthesia and everything else. People line up and say, "Please take me to do this surgery." They fly in from other parts of the country. They don't ask, "How much is it going to cost for you to perform your miracle work on my shoulder and preserve my arm and my shoulder for the rest of my life?" They don't care.

Fortunately, I am properly insured, but it's the same thing. If your product makes a difference to this person, they're more concerned with how they can get it, and when and how fast. The payment comes later. As they say, if a person really wants your product or service, they will find a way to pay for it.

The fourth part of a marketing strategy is *concentration*, and *concentration* is one of the most important of all words in business life. This is where you concentrate all of your time, efforts, advertising, promotion—remember we're talking about marketing, which is attracting prospective customers. You concentrate just on those people who most want and most need and are most willing to pay for your product or service the fastest.

Last year about $20 billion was spent on marketing research. Marketing research is basically asking people questions. Are you the appropriate person for this? They check your income and your background and your work and your occupation and your education.

For example, we just bought a building called the Publisher Building in one of our real-estate developments. This person publishes magazines on boating, expensive boats, yachts. Whom do they send the magazine to? Whom do they sell subscriptions to? People who own boats, people who have boats, people who have already bellied up to the bar and paid a lot of money for boats. Those are the places where you concentrate your advertising and promotion—on people who buy and own boats.

Again, here are the big four: Number one, specialize. Where do you specialize? And remember, you must be able to explain it to a child.

Number two is the most important part of advertising, the heartbeat of business—your area of competitive advantage. In what way is your product or service superior to that of anyone else? And in what way is it so important that people will prefer to buy it, and even pay more for it?

Number three is segmentation. Of all the millions of people in the market, who exactly are those people who are closest to buying your product or service? They want it, they need it, they can use it, they can afford it. It's superior to anything else that anybody wants. In fact, people line up to pay enormous amounts of money to buy the product, and they wait for months for it to become available, because that's the one they want.

Finally, concentration. You concentrate all of your efforts all day, every day on just those people who can buy your product or service the fastest. That's 600 pages from Michael Porter. That's a library shelf full of books. That's a graduate degree.

I have a friend who has a master's degree from a major university. It's basically on marketing and competitive advantage, because it's so important to all businesses. Lack of clarity with regard to those answers is the primary reason for failure in marketing and business. You advertise in the wrong places. You offer the wrong appeals. You go to the wrong people, and as a result, your store sits empty.

Next, you have to create a culture of sales in your company, so that everybody realizes that sales are vital to your business, and customers are vital to sales. Good companies, from the boss all the way down, love their customers. They treat them with respect. They treat them as though they're here to bring suitcases full of money. Everybody in the company treats their customers well.

There's a saying that if staff or sales people do not treat customers well, it's because the boss doesn't treat them well. It always filters down from the top. You can always tell how people at the top feel about customers by the way everybody treats customers all the way down.

The best companies love their customers. Once they get a customer, they will never lose that customer. They will take care of that customer. They do anything for their customers. They bend over backwards. They will give refunds and replacements. It's not a matter of the money. It's a matter of customer loyalty, because the customer is so important to them.

If you are offtrack in any area in selling, that alone can cause you to be unsuccessful. Rather than talk about the sales process, which is a matter of two-, three-, four-day seminars, we can say that in sales there are seven key requirements. If any one of these is off, it can cost you the sale and ultimately the business. We call them *the seven P's*. If your sales go down, you have to look at the seven P's. If there's one flaw in those seven P's, it can cause your sales to go down, cause your sales to collapse, cause your company to go bankrupt.

The Seven P's of Sales

1. Product
2. Promotion
3. Price
4. Place
5. Positioning
6. Packaging
7. People

Number one is the *product.* If your sales are down, the first thing you have to do is look at your product. Is my product the appropriate product for the market today? Is what I am selling based on the pillars of marketing strategy? Is what I'm selling what people want and need and are willing to pay for?

Because things are moving so fast on a regular basis, sometimes every week, every month in our business we launch a whole new sales program. We have ten or twenty people working on a whole new program, developing the product, and making sure that the product is what people want. If, for any reason it doesn't sell, we immediately jerk it off the market and fix it or replace it. It's almost like running out of oxygen: you move fast. Is this product correct? You can almost guarantee 100 percent of the time whatever product you have will soon become the wrong product.

Sometimes it'll become the wrong product overnight. I mentioned Krispy Kreme donuts. It was the hottest-selling donut in the history of the world; within a few weeks, it was off the market, and the Krispy Kreme donut stores were all empty and bankrupt. Why did this happen? They fell in love with their product, and they refused to change it. People were ready to go; the stores were there. Why didn't they put in a product that was more attractive? I guess it was lack of imagination, lack of confidence, the comfort zone. They were comfortable doing something. It didn't work anymore, and they didn't replace it.

So number one is the product. If your sales are down, the first thing you look at is whether your product is the right product.

Number two is *promotion*—how you sell the product. What are your methods of selling and distribution? What are your methods of advertising and attracting new people? What is your sales process? What do you offer to get people to buy your product immediately rather than wait?

One of the most powerful turning points in a company's business is changing the sales process so that it's much more attractive than it was before. They're constantly improving the sales process. If you're not making sales, you use the magic words *I am responsible. I am responsible.* Either my product is no longer what people want more than anything else, or maybe we're not selling it or offering it in such a way that people want to buy it now.

Remember, a persuasive sales presentation has the effect of "I want it now." They listen to you and say, "I like it. I'll take it now," and they'll say yes before they ask the price. If people start to quibble about price before they even understand your offering, it means that something's seriously wrong with what you're doing.

Make a single change in your product lineup, or a single change in the way you promote, and you could totally transform your business, sometimes for good, and sometimes for ill. Over the years, J.C. Penney, one of the most successful department-store chains in the United States, had developed the philosophy of having really great sales on a regular basis. People who went to J.C. Penney knew

---

Remember, a persuasive sales presentation
has the effect of "I want it now."

---

that they could get good-quality products manufactured by the best manufacturers. On a regular basis, usually every month, sometimes every week, the stores would have a special sale that would bring people in by the busload.

Some great genius at headquarters decided that the world had changed. This was the old philosophy of J.C. Penney, so they were going to have a new philosophy. They hired the gentleman who had established the Apple stores. The Apple stores are the highest-grossing stores per square foot in the history of the world. Brilliant.

They brought this man in, and he said, "OK, I'm going to change our method of marketing. We're going to stop all sales. No more sales. We're going to offer higher-quality, higher-priced products. We're going to have different ways of promotion and in-store activities and so on. He's going to do a clean sweep and move into the next generation."

Within a year, J.C. Penney was almost bankrupt. People who were accustomed to going to the store on the basis of their methods of promotion and product service lines said, "The heck with this," and they went somewhere else. Remember, it's not as if there are no places to go to buy clothes and department-store products and services.

The board of directors had to fire this guy and go back and get the previous president, who had built and run the company for years and who, they'd felt, was too old-school, stodgy. He had done the same thing week after week, month after month—good-quality products, sales and bonuses, and so on.

They went back and brought this guy out of retirement, and they asked him to take over the company. He came back in and installed the methods of marketing and sales that had worked for 100 years. J.C. Penney had been written off by the big financial advisors; they said, "It's over. They've had their day in the sun." By turning around, going right back to the basics that made them successful—as we say, dance with the one that brung you—the company turned around. Their customers came back out of loyalty: hundreds, thousands, of families were accustomed to the J.C. Penney way. It was almost like a member of the family. The sales went up 50 percent, and moved from massive losses, almost bankruptcy, into profit. They're in profit again today.

So small changes in promotion can totally transform the results of the business. You have to have the courage to admit whatever you're doing now is not working. It's not generating sales. That's your measure.

If you go into a medical office, the first thing they do is take your pulse and your blood pressure, because your pulse and your blood pressure will tell a lot about your physical health. Then they measure your temperature, and those three will tell them 95 percent of what they need to know about your body. In business, it's just one thing. It's sales. Are you making sales, and profitable sales, and taking money home at the end of the day?

The third P is the *price*. Small changes in price can dramatically change the attractiveness of the product. You see companies like McDonald's and J.C. Penney, which are having problems. They go to a new pricing structure with special bonuses and rewards and discounts.

J.C. Penney went back to the old way, which people were accustomed to.

I built a business importing Japanese vehicles from Japan, and I set up fifty-four dealerships selling the vehicles. One was a van-like vehicle. We had bought several million dollars' worth, and they were all sitting there at the dock, because people weren't buying them. The geniuses in the business above me said, "We have to sell them off. We have to get rid of them. We have to cut the prices, bite the bullet, cut our losses, and lose money."

I said, "Wait a minute. Why don't we add a special winch so that you can go up mountainsides? Why don't we add a special rack on the top so that you can go camping with these? Why don't we add heavy bumpers so that you can climb up and down mountains?"

Add $1,000 worth of products at wholesale; install them. Add $2,000 to the price, and put the vehicles on the market. So we did. We sold them all within two weeks, because we called this model the Prospector. Where did we sell it? In mountainous regions. We sold it in regions where the idea of being able to go over almost any kind of terrain and up steep hills was important. You could drive down a river and camp with your family. There was nothing like it.

Instead of cutting the price and wiping out all of our profits for the last year, we raised the price and generated $25 million in sales. People said, "This is crazy." It's crazy, but it worked.

If people are afraid that the prices are too high, the automatic response is to cut the price. But maybe not.

Maybe you add something new or different to make it more attractive, even at a higher price, and people end up buying it.

You study the price, and you study whether you should increase it. Should you lower it? Should you combine it? Should we have an add-on to the product or service?

The fourth P is *place*. What is the place where the customer acquires the product or service? Is this the right place? Are enough people walking in the door? Is your phone ringing? Are people coming into your place of business to buy it? Maybe you need to change the location.

Many years ago, a woman grew up in a nice Mormon family in Salt Lake City. Her mother was a wonderful cook, and she made beautiful cookies. She used butter in all of her cookies, so they were delicious. She loved to make cookies, and the woman studied at the elbow of her mother.

The woman had five children. The fifth was finally old enough to go to school every day, so she had time on her hands. People were always saying, "You should bake these cookies and make them available. You should sell them."

The woman finally decided to open a cookie store. She found a little cookie store with an oven in it down in a side street near the main street. So she opened up the store, she made the cookies, she put her sign up, but nobody walked down the side street. It was a little arty side street, and nobody went down it.

The woman had these beautiful cookies, and no customers. Instead of being passive, she took the cookies, cut them up, walked down to the main street, where all the foot traffic was, and offered samples. "Here, try these cookies." People would casually stop and pick them, and say, "Geez, this is a good cookie. This is delicious."

"You can get all you want down at my store, down the alley."

People began to stream down the alley. She realized that, especially for a retail product like this, the location was crucial. You could have the finest cookies in the world, but if nobody came past or came into your store, nothing would happen.

The woman rented a second store, and this time it was on the main street. She paid vastly more. They tried to convince her that she should go cheap on the rent. "You should get a cheap place." "Yes, but if you have a cheap place that nobody comes to, you go broke."

She put a cookie store on the main street, and people started to come in, but not enough. So she said, "What can we do?" Her brother, who was a plumber, said, "Why don't we take the piping from the cookie oven and put in an outlet from the piping onto the sidewalk in front of the store?"

People would walk along, not paying attention, and they would walk into this beautiful smell of these delicious cookies, like their mother used to make. Holy smokes. They started to stream into the store. Then the woman found that people were highly visual. She reorganized the front of the store so that there were samples of cookies in beautiful trays at a very steep angle. A steep angle, beautiful smell, lovely cookies.

Her name was Debbi Fields. She built a chain of almost 500 stores and sold it for almost half a billion dollars. The first time I heard about her, I was on the island of Maui in Hawaii. I asked some people, "What are you doing tomorrow?"

"We're flying over to the main island to get cookies," they said.

"Cookies?"

"Yes, there's only one store, Debbi Fields' store, and we have to get these cookies."

They were flying over, and they were paying. The whole family went over by plane to the main island to buy cookies.

"Can you get me a couple of cookies?" I said.

"You don't buy a couple of cookies; you buy boxes full."

"Buy me a boxful."

They came back, and those cookies were extraordinary. Everybody would look at them and envy them because the cookies were so great. People were flying from all over the Hawaiian islands into Honolulu to go to the Debbi Fields store. Eventually they had buses coming from the airport, bringing in the customers, and taking them back to the airport. They had Debbi Fields flights from different islands, which is extraordinary.

Another example: Ray Kroc, founder of McDonald's, would spend any amount of money to buy a location. He would always buy them on main concourses in shopping areas, and he always bought the real estate. He realized that McDonald's is not primarily in the hamburger business, it's in the real-estate business. They own more choice commercial real estate around the world, by billions and billions of dollars, than anybody else in history. Ray Kroc realized that if you bought this beautiful com-

---

McDonald's is not primarily in the hamburger business;
it's in the real-estate business.

---

mercial property at main intersections, it could only go up in value. Populations would increase.

Place is important. People rent or lease a space, and by the time the lease is up, they could be forced out or forced to pay twice as much. I've worked with lots of business owners who leased a piece of property and made the business really successful. Then the owner of the property came back and tripled their rent, and they could no longer stay in business. By this time, this was such a popular area that they were able to rent it overnight to someone else.

Number five is *positioning*. Positioning is what people say about you and your business—your reputation. How are you positioned in the marketplace? What do people say? What are the words they use? This is what they discovered in all the work on positioning: what are the words that people use to describe your business?

If someone asks about you as a person or about your business, what words pop into mind? Honest, intelligent, highly competent, warm, friendly, dependable?

Then, what words do you *want* people to use? If people used these words when they thought about you or your product or service, would they help you make more sales?

Of course, the easiest word to pick is the *best*, but then you have to ask, the best in what terms? How do you define *good*, *better*, *best* in terms of a product or service? Sometimes, as we said before, it's as simple as delivering the product faster. It's as simple as being friendlier than anybody else. It's as simple as being polite. It doesn't have to be something great, especially if it's a product that's available elsewhere.

So you ask, how am I positioned in the marketplace, and how do I need to be positioned to be seen as the best in the business? You never do or say anything that is inconsistent with your chosen image. This is your positioning. This is your reputation. This is how people think and feel about you.

With regard to positioning and reputation, I came across a definition of branding some years ago, which almost knocked me off my chair, because it was the best single article on branding I'd ever read. It was only a page and a half long.

What is a brand? A brand, according to the article, is two things. A brand is the promise you make when you ask a person to buy your product or service, and a brand is the promise that you keep after they've bought your product or service. This is a revolutionary concept: the promise you make, the promise you keep.

What promise do you make when you ask a person to buy your product or service, and what promise do you deliver? The promise that you deliver determines the entire future of your business. It has to be clear.

They say that if you go to this restaurant, the food is great. The service is wonderful. You'll have a really enjoyable evening. Then you go there, and you get exactly that—beautiful food, beautiful service, nice people. They lured you in with the promise, and then they delivered on their promise.

All successful companies are companies that promise things that people want very much, and then they deliver on their promises. This is positioning. Again, you have to come back to clarity. You know the 80/20 rules that keeps biting you in the bum—80 percent of business owners don't know the answers to these questions.

What does your company stand for? What is your positioning? What do people say about you and your product or service when you're not there? That's going to determine whether they buy and whether other people buy.

Number six is *packaging*. Packaging is the visual appearance that your product or service has for customers and prospective customers. Many companies have found that they have a really excellent product, but it has poor packaging. Earlier in the game, somebody didn't want to spend a lot of money on letterhead or packaging or boxing, and they don't understand why people take one look at their business and walk away.

I explained this concept to a couple of my clients in my coaching program, and they went away. The program was a full day for every ninety days. The clients, a husband and wife, came back, and we discussed what they had applied. They said, "We want to tell you our story."

They had built a successful business out of their home, offering financial and investment and insurance services. He started off working for another company, and he felt he could do it better on his own.

The business was doing reasonably well, and they were quite happy. Most times he would go to clients' homes or places of business. Sometimes people would come to his house. They finally decided to move to an office, because they were having too many people coming in; it was not legal under the zoning laws. They moved to an office.

Then the wife said, "Our business has dropped off, and we're struggling for business. People come into our office. They are polite, and they look around, and they walk out and don't come back. Our closing ratio is terrible."

"Let me guess," I said. "When you moved from your home to your new office, you took the same furniture with you to save money."

"How did you know that?"

"Because that's what all entrepreneurs do. They think nobody notices, so you took old furniture, old carpets, paintings from the basement or the garage, and you put them up. People come in. The first thing they hear is what I call the canary song—*cheap, cheap, cheap.* You're asking these people to entrust you with their money and their financial future, and you look poor. You look cheap. Why don't you take a few thousand dollars and invest in your office—beautiful paintings, beautiful carpeting, a music system, and so on? See what happens."

They came back to the next session ninety days later, and they were beaming. Their closing ratio from customers who had followed up on their advertising and come to their office had been struggling: one out of ten people would become a client, and not even a big client. Now the closing ratio was four or five out of ten.

The husband said, "It's astonishing. People walk in, and almost always the first thing they say is, 'These are really nice offices.'" In psychology it's called the *halo effect*. If your offices are attractive and look expensive, everything about your company is considered to be of higher quality. Your work is considered to be of higher quality. The results that you'll get will be of higher quality. They said, "We have tripled and quadrupled the size of our business in the last ninety days."

By the way, I offer people double-double. If you don't double your income and double your time off, you don't have to pay. You get your money back. This is another example of why I never have to give people their money back: sometimes it's just one idea, like making their facility more attractive. Remember, human beings are extremely visual, and whatever they see reverberates in their subconscious, their emotions, their decision making, their trust. Make sure that everything that your customer sees is attractive.

I had a young man, about twenty-eight years old, working hard in real estate. He was wearing a beard that was almost like a professorial beard. He would make appointments and get listings and do things on the phone. Then he'd go and see the clients, and their enthusiasm would die away.

He asked me why. "I work so hard, but I simply can't make any money. I meet with a customer, and the customer just decides not to work with me."

"According to the research, it's because when you wear a beard, you're considered to have something to hide," I

In business, practice the *halo effect*: If your offices are attractive and look expensive, everything about your company is considered to be of higher quality.

---

said. "You're considered to be dishonest, like a masked robber in the old days."

It's an unconscious decision. It's not something that the person calculates on a piece of paper. They see you, and they automatically don't trust you enough to do business. Oh, they like you, and they talk to you, but they don't trust you enough to entrust their money to you.

"This is my personality," he said. He was—*pissy* is the best word for it. "This is my personality, this is the way I express my uniqueness."

I said, "That's fine. You can continue to do that as long as you want to be poor. You're choosing to be poor, and you're choosing to be unsuccessful."

I got a letter from him a month later. He had thought about it, and he realized I was right. He went out and got a professional haircut, and instead of wearing open-necked shirts, he wore a suit. He looked good. He said his business exploded. He did more business in the next thirty days then he'd done in the last year. He said he couldn't believe the impact visual appearance makes.

When IBM started off, they were absolutely adamant. They could see that 99 percent of their success, their sales, were going to be determined by how customers felt about their salespeople. They had to make sure that their sales-people looked good, and they developed a dress code right from the beginning. It was a dark-blue suit, a white shirt, a dark tie, and polished black shoes, with a conservative haircut. (At that time, it was almost all men selling.) So when you met an IBM person, he looked great.

A friend of mine got hired at IBM. He went into work in an old suit that he'd gotten for his high-school graduation.

His boss said to him, "What on earth is that?"

"What do you mean?"

"What are you wearing?"

"This is my suit."

The boss said, "You're not wearing that in this office. In this office, you dress like an IBM person."

My friend, said, "All right. I'll get a new suit. I'll change tomorrow."

"No, you'll do it now. You'll go now."

"I don't even know where to buy an expensive suit."

"You go down to Harry's Tailors on Third Street."

So my friend left the office; this was about 10:00 in the morning. He went down to Harry's Tailors, and Harry walked in. He said, "You from IBM?" He got the new guys every single time. The manager sent them down.

My friend bought a beautiful suit. He said it transformed his career. Earlier in IBM history, you'd have to dress really well on your first day. He eventually became a sales manager, had a very large team under him. With almost half the people, he had to give the talk, the lecture about how you have to look great.

One of the best compliments I ever had—I still remember it, and I've had it more than once—was when a senior executive in a hotel said, "You look like you're from IBM."

I've always dressed well. I was tutored in proper dress at an early part of my career, so every single time I appeared with business people, I always dressed well, as well as or better than the senior managers.

I knew it was important. I didn't know how important it was until that senior IBM executive said, "You dress like IBM. You dress like the kind of people that we want to put in front of our audiences." That led to thirty engagements at the highest fees that IBM paid at that time, so it was a lot.

So look at everything. The rule is, everything counts. If it doesn't help, it hurts. Think about your clients. How do your clients dress? How do they appear? How do they groom? What kind of clothes do they wear? You have to dress so that they respect you and esteem you and value you.

I've had many experiences over the years when I've taken people aside and told them very gently, "If you want to be successful, you have to change your appearance. You don't look like a successful person." Some of them have gotten very angry with me. Some were resentful, but so many of them—I have a whole file full of stories—came back and said, "That piece of advice changed my life. I had no idea. I came from an average family. My father never wore a suit. I didn't know anybody else who wore suits. It never dawned on me that how I looked on the outside was affecting how people assessed me on the inside."

Number seven is *people*. In sales and marketing, it's the people who interact with the customer. Some years ago, SAS, Scandinavian Airlines System, got into serious financial trouble. It was losing a lot of money, so they threw out the old president and the old executive group, and they brought in a man named Jan Carlzon. Jan Carlzon was an older executive with a great reputation. They put him in charge, and he turned the company around almost completely.

He discovered that the primary creator of reputation, whether or not people flew with the airline, was the SAS staff with whom they dealt on telephone and at check-in counters. He said, "Every single time a prospective flyer comes into contact with an SAS staff member, it is a moment of truth."

Carlzon wrote a book called *Moments of Truth*. Everybody in that company was trained to make every moment of truth a really happy moment. Every executive was required to work for at least one full day checking bags in airports all over Europe. They had to check bags, and they also had to work as stewards on the planes and serve coffee and water and food. They had talked to people and asked, "Are you enjoying your experience? Is there anything we can do to make it better for you?" They rotated around so that everybody in the company was constantly forced to work face-to-face, knee-to-knee with their customers.

It used to be if there was a problem with luggage or a flyer or something else, an employee would have to go to the supervisor and ask what to do. Carlzon said, "Eliminate that step. From now on, you use your own good judgment to take care of our flyers. If they have a problem, solve the problem. If they have a difficulty with a suitcase or a seat or anything else, solve it right there at the counter. When the person leaves the counter, their problem is solved. Create happy moments of truth."

I could spend days on this subject. Your job and your business is to make every single point of contact a moment of truth, and make it so that people feel really happy that they spoke to you. They come to you with problems and difficulties, which occur inevitably, but you take care of it immediately.

If you do that, people remember that moment of truth as a moment of warmth, as a moment of happiness. "My problem, my stress, my strain was taken away." They come back like a ball on a rubber string. They keep coming back over and over to you.

So that's the sales process: the seven P's. Keep looking at each one of those seven areas. What is it about your product? Is it the right product at the right time at the right place? What about your pricing? Is it the right price for this market, for your competition, for your customers?

What about your promotion, the way that you market and sell and attract people? Is it working? Is your place of business a good choice?

Look at probably the greatest business success story in the world today, which is Amazon. Amazon started off by selling books online. Now they are reverse-engineering, and they're opening up physical bookstores in almost

---

Your job and your business is to make every single point of contact a moment of truth, and make it so that people feel really happy that they spoke to you.

---

every major area. They're going right back to the top of the waterfall, and they are reverse-engineering everything, because it makes it more convenient. You can go into an Amazon store if you have a proper number, like Uber. You can walk around, you can buy all the stuff, and you can walk out. It's automatically calculated on the computer. Why? Because that's what people want. It's making it easier and easier and faster and faster for you.

They asked, what are the most popular products that sell the very most, that people consume over and over again? They make those available immediately. They don't try to offer all their products in the stores. They don't offer all sizes. They'll offer one size of a very popular product, and they'll make it available so you can whip in and whip out and get it. You can actually send them a message and arrive five minutes afterwards, and they'll have someone come straight out of the store and put it in your car. You drive away.

It's like a juggernaut. How do you stop a company that has this obsession with customer service? It's constantly looking for ways to make those moments of truth happy moments of truth.

As I've said, in my coaching programs for business owners, I guarantee double-double. You'll double your income, double your time off. On my first day, I teach them a series of techniques, and it doesn't take a year. Within seven days to one month, people's incomes have already taken off, so I'm going to give you the most important things I teach.

Steps for Immediate Action

1. Get a spiral notebook and write down your top ten goals every day.
2. More, less, stop, start. What should I do more of, less of, stop, or start?
3. Zero-based thinking.

For the first step, *get a spiral notebook,* like a school notebook, *and write down your top ten goals every day.* For example, "I earn X number of dollars in 2019." You write it down as a present-tense statement, as though it is already a reality and is taking place.

With this, your subconscious mind can work on it twenty-four hours a day. Your subconscious mind has a special technology that only allows it to work on activities that are positive and are phrased in the present tense.

Next, select your most important goal, and every single day do something on your most important goal. Write down your top ten goals; next day come back, open the book, write down ten goals without looking at your previous ones. Don't copy. This is not a copybook: each time you rewrite your ten goals, they will be different, and they will penetrate deeper and deeper into your subconscious.

Eventually these goals will activate your superconscious. Your superconscious mind is a power that you have and that all successful people use to become rich. They do it with constant clarity—writing and rewriting their goals so their subconscious and superconscious are working on them twenty-four hours a day. Clarity is really important.

If you write your goals down, the definition of them will change, sometimes by one word, sometimes by one comma. They'll become clearer and clearer, and you'll start to move faster and faster towards your goals, and your goals will start to move towards you.

I've found that the only way you can improve your life or work is by changing something. I call this second step *more, less, stop, start.* These are four keys to making productive changes in your business for the rest of your life. I like to reframe each of these words as questions.

Question number one is, *what should I do more of*? What's working the best in my business?

People say, "Some things I do are really working well. Some things I do are not working that well. So I'll divide my time amongst the activities, 50/50, so every activity gets a little share of my time."

No. It's what should I do *more* of. One of the great questions in time management is what can I, and only I, do that, if done well, will make a real difference in my business? That's what I should do more of all the time. What's giving me my best results now?

Question number two is, *what should I do less of*? What should I curtail? The answer is, do fewer of those things that are not giving you the results that you want. You pull back on them and spend more time doing the things that are giving you the best results.

Question number three is, *what should I start doing that I'm not doing now*? I'm going to have to start doing five or ten or a hundred things in the course of my career, but because of the comfort zone, the hardest thing for the human psyche is to do something new and different, to start doing something that you've never done before.

The principal reason businesses struggle is that they cannot get up enough momentum to start doing something they haven't done before. They keep slipping back into the comfort zone. They keep delaying and procrastinating. This could have to do with bringing in a new product or service, discontinuing an old product or service, hiring a new person, or firing a current employee.

You keep asking, "What do I need to start doing and start doing quickly in order to succeed today?" There's always an answer to that. Whatever you're doing today, if part of it is obsolete, you shouldn't be doing it at all, which brings us to question number four. *What should I stop doing altogether?* In every business, there are some things that you are doing that seemed like a good idea, and they may have given you great results at a certain time, but now you should stop doing them.

The third step is worth this entire course. I call it *zero-based thinking*. Zero-based thinking comes from zero-based accounting. The man who invented zero-based accounting is still a legend in the accounting industry, if there is such a thing. He came up with this concept:

Four Questions for making positive changes in your business:

1. What should I do more of?
2. What should I do less of?
3. What should I start doing that I'm not doing now?
4. What should I stop doing altogether?

Rather than increasing or decreasing the expenditures in a particular area in a company every three, six, nine, twelve months, every accounting period, ask whether we should be spending money in this area at all. Look at every expenditure as though it were a brand-new expenditure. That totally transformed the way people looked at their books, their financing, their accounting, their future activities.

For an individual, zero-based thinking asks this question, and this is the golden question: is there anything that I am doing today that, knowing what I now know, I would not start up again today if I had to do it over? I call this a KWINK analysis, K-W-I-N-K, *knowing what I now know*. Is there anything that I'm doing that, if I could start it over again, I would not do it, not get into at all?

If there is, the next question is, how do you get out and how fast? Move quickly. Don't delay, don't procrastinate, don't wait for next week or next month. It's just like when we say that if you have a person in your company, and you realize this person is not working out, let them go immediately. Today. Not this afternoon, not after lunch. Once you've made the decision, once it crosses your mind that you would not hire this person back again today based on your experience with this person, then cut your losses immediately.

You then go through your entire life. There are three main types of relationships in your life: personal relationships, professional relationships, business relationships. Eighty-five percent of all your problems in life will come from problems with your relationships, and they will

---

The *Zero-Based Thinking* Question: Knowing what I now know, is there anything that we're doing in this company that we would not start up again today?

---

be situations that you know you shouldn't be in and you should get out of. So whatever it is, whatever you're doing at this minute, stop and go and end the relationship. I've given this advice to millions of people. They come back and say they couldn't believe what happened to their life afterwards, and it was always good.

When you finally decide to stop doing something or to get out of a bad relationship, you're going to have two responses. The first is, "I should have done this a long time ago. Why did I wait so long?" The second response you're going to have is one of freedom and exhilaration. You're going to feel happy, almost joyous, almost like you're on dope of some kind, because you feel so happy when you finally cut it off and eliminate it and walk away completely.

The second area has to do with anything in your business. I've taken hundreds, thousands of business owners through this, and every one of them comes up with gems, golden ideas that have business-transforming effects. We go through the products. Is there any product or service that you are offering today that, knowing what you know, you would not offer anymore? You would not bring it to the market because the market demand is not there. Or the competition is too stiff.

General Electric spent years building a worldwide multi-divisional set of companies, and they decided to cut back to four. They said, "We're making profits on all of these companies, but we can never be a world leader. We can never make really big profits, but they consume enormous resources in terms of time, people, money." So they decided to reduce the size of their company dramatically and get out of major industries that they'd spent decades building.

You know that happened? When they announced this, their stocks boomed. They jumped because the owners cheered: "Yes, that's true. You can make a profit, but if you had all of your resources in these four areas, this is where you're breaking the bank at Monte Carlo."

GE had spent decades building their business, and now they were going to cut back very quickly in every area, because they wouldn't get into that area again today if they had to do it over.

So look at all of your products, look at your services, look at your pricing, look at your customers.

Successful companies commonly fire their worst customers every year. They sit down with their customers, and they analyze the account. How much did the people buy? How much profit do we earn on what they buy? How much hassle does this customer require? Are they good payers?

They cut off the bottom 10 or 20 percent of their customers. To get rid of their bad customers, they tell them, "We're going to raise your prices between 20 percent and 50 percent next year" because of their pricing structure, changes, and everything else. The customers walk away.

There's no animosity, and there's no negativity. They just fire their customers.

You can look at any process—advertising or promotion or fundraising—any markets that are local or national or international, anybody that you're dealing with. Ask yourself, would you get into this business again if you had to do it over?

I spoke in Brazil in the last couple of years, three or four days each time. Brazil is one of the biggest countries in the world, 200 million people. A few years ago, Walmart went into Brazil gangbusters. They attacked like the Marines at Guadalcanal and bought several hundred stores all over the country. Then they brought in the Walmart method and so on.

After about five years, they realized that the Brazilian mentality, Brazilian market, Brazilian pricing, sales, competition was not a good mix for them. So they announced they were walking away. People jeered at them for making a big business mistake, but they said, "We realized we've made a mistake. It seemed like a good idea at the time, but knowing what we now know about the Brazilian market and competition, we would not make that decision, so we're walking away."

Walmart did the same thing in Germany. They aggressively went after new markets, but after a bad experience, they realized it wasn't a good choice, so they had the courage to make the hard decisions. They had the courage to stand back from previous decisions and walk away. This is the most important quality for leaders.

There's a type of executive in the United States that I've spent some time with. They're never seen or heard. Very seldom do they ever get into the papers. They're called *turnaround specialists*.

Let's say a company is in serious trouble. Sales, profitability, everything is down. An executive who gets a company into trouble is not capable of getting it out, because of the comfort zone. That executive cannot make the hard decisions necessary to turn the company around, so the company has to get rid of them and bring in someone who's really hard, someone who has no emotion.

The turnaround specialist did not build the company. They did not start the company. They have only one goal: to make the company profitable. So they come in and they apply zero-based thinking to every part of the business. Knowing what I now know, is there anything that we're doing in this company that we would not start up again today?

Whenever you see in the paper that a company has changed management or appointed a new president, and then a few weeks later, they've laid off 10,000 people, they closed ten factories, and they shut down 600 stores, they have brought in an outside person, a hired gun.

I've worked with these specialists, and they've said that it's very simple. First, they go through the entire company, and every single person in the company, with a KWINK analysis. They talk to people. Would we hire this person back again? They go through every person in a division, and they sit down with the senior management. OK, here's the person, name, background, history. Would we hire this person if they applied for their job again today? If the answer is no, out, out, out. Finally somebody has the courage and the resolution to make the hard decisions that, in some companies, should have been made a long time ago. The old executive rode the poor previous decision into bankruptcy because they didn't have the courage to cut it off, cut their losses.

Then you go through investments. You go through any other commitment that you have in your life. The critical factor is stress. What in your life is causing you stress? Whatever it is, you examine it. You hold it up to the light and say, would I get into this again today if I had to do it over again? If the answer is no, how do I get out and how fast?

You need to use this as a go-forward tool in your life, especially in your business. In a small or medium-sized growing business, in a rapidly changing economy, you have to be asking this all the time. Whenever you run up against a wall, whenever you have a problem, whenever the product stops selling, whenever you have incompetent people in place, whenever the sales or the profits slow down, you immediately stop everything. Stop the clock. Would we get into this again if we had to do it over? Then have the courage to get out and get out quickly.

Many people are turnaround specialists on their own account. For example, Mitt Romney and Bain & Company. They are venture capitalists. They go in and buy a company that is in serious trouble but has great potential.

Why don't the owners or the management of the company solve the problem? They don't have the courage. They want to just keep things going and hope that something will happen. They pray for miracles.

There was a book that came out a few years ago whose title is worth the price: *Hope Is Not a Strategy*. An enormous number of businesses are using hope as their primary strategy for success.

Mitt Romney and his people find a company that's highly undervalued because it's mismanaged. They come in and buy the company at a very good price. Then they get rid of all the old people and discontinue the bottom 80 percent of products and services that are not that profitable. Then they throw all of their resources into making the top 20 percent of products even more profitable. They reduce costs and expenses. They increase sales and profitability. They do this over and over again. They save thousands of jobs. They save dozens of factories. They keep entire cities open. They save careers and everything else, and at the end of the day the stock goes up two, three, four, five times.

I've worked with these people, I've spent time with them, and they've told me their stories of what they've done. They're absolutely wonderful, because they have the financial ability to go in and buy the company, discontinue everything that they would not do, and turn the company around over and over to the tune of hundreds of millions and then billions. BlackRock, one of the greatest turnaround companies in history, is now managing a trillion dollars' worth of assets all over the world. They started off with a couple of people and an idea, and they bought a small company.

So have the courage to ask, what are the stress points in my business? What are the areas where I'm under a lot of stress, I'm unhappy, I'm not making progress? If I were not in this area today, would I get into it again? If the answer is no, get out as fast as you can.

So those are my three recommendations: *very clear goals*; *ask the four questions, more of, less of, start*, or *stop*—and *zero-based thinking.* If you were not already doing something in your life that's causing you stress or unhappiness, would you start it up again today? If the answer is no, get out as fast as you can.

Let me just add a few things in conclusion. First, there are more opportunities for more people to be successful in business than have ever existed in all of human history, except for tomorrow and next week and next month and next year. There's no lack of opportunity.

Most of the most successful businesses in the world today were started at the bottom of the worst recessions. Apple started at the bottom of a recession. Google started at the bottom of a recession. Microsoft started at the bottom of a recession.

IBM started in 1928. They just were coming up to the end of the runway to take off, and the entire economy collapsed for ten or twenty years. When the dust had settled, they were one of the biggest and fastest-growing companies in business. Someone asked Thomas J. Watson Sr., the CEO, why he was advertising for salespeople in the middle of the Depression. "Why are you doing this? Every other company is firing and laying off everybody."

"I'm in my fifties now," he said, "and at my age, some people who are successful become eccentric, and they drink too much or they take dope or they chase girls. Well, my eccentricity is I like to hire salespeople."

That's all he did. He hired salespeople, and the salespeople went out and made sales and generated business activity. While everybody else was cutting back, by the time the dust had settled, he had founded one of the biggest and most profitable companies.

People say, "Oh, it's the economy." There's a line from one of the great philosophers that says, "Remember that in times like this, there have always been times like this." Therefore the opportunities for you are unlimited.

The second thing is, you can learn anything you need to learn to be successful in a business. I have seen this with people who built hundred-million-dollar and even billion-dollar fortunes. They started off with nothing and they knew nothing about a particular industry except they had heard that it was a good one. So they began to do their research. They studied for hours, and they went to conferences, and they asked people, and they began to assemble knowledge. Before you knew it, they began to move up in that industry and soon became giants.

I worked with a man who read my book many years ago, when the Soviet Union fell. He was pushing a gurney at a hospital in St. Petersburg. He found that he could never be successful working in a hospital, so he began to sell stuff. He would buy things for cheap, and he would go out and sell them. He would make some money and buy some more and do it over again.

Finally, he left the hospital. Over time, he learned about a particular natural resource, potash, which is essential for many types of manufacturing, such as fertilizer and steel. He began to study it. There was enormous confusion in the potash industry worldwide. Before the dust had settled, he owned the second-largest potash company in the world and became one of the richest men in history.

This man was pushing a gurney when he started. He and I talked about the fact that you can learn anything you need to learn if you see an area where there's a possible opportunity. There's no guarantee, but sometimes if you see an area and you put your whole heart into learning everything about that area, you find an opportunity that nobody else had seen, and it enables you to make more progress in a year or two than many other people could make in an entire lifetime.

I read in the newspapers about income and inequality and lack of productivity, but the bottom line is that people who are learning and growing are creating and seeing opportunities continually. In fact, at a certain point they have so many opportunities that they don't know where to start and where to stop.

There are so many things going on, so when you see an opportunity, throw your whole heart into learning everything that you possibly can in that area, and then throw your whole heart into taking a chance. Roll the dice—Texas hold'em. Go all in, and see what happens. You don't have to break the bank. You don't have to risk everything you have, but just continually push forward, push forward, and push forward. Never hold back.

The third thing to remember is that you can do it. You have more capabilities than you could use in a hundred lifetimes. Learn more and more and practice and study. Start a little earlier, stay a little later.

Fourth is make a decision never to give up. You're never going to give up. You're going to keep on working. You'll try this, you'll try that, you'll try this, you'll try that.

Let me wrap up with a story that has to do with why people succeed in business. One of the top universities in the United States is Babson College. You can get a master's degree two or three years after you have graduated.

There's a professor there, Dr. Robert Ronstadt. He did a thirteen-year study to see what happened to people who took the MBA. Part of the degree was to actually design and start and build a company—to go through every single thing that we've talked about and many things besides, so that they really had a great in-depth knowledge of every-thing they needed.

They found out that 90 percent of the people who got this degree never used it. They went to work for a larger com-pany. They worked for wages, went back to work for their family company, and so on. Only 10 percent actually used the degree. Of these, a very high percentage succeeded.

The researchers asked these people what they did. They found that the turning point in success was when they decided to start a business. Then they launched. This was the turning point: they decided they were going to start a business, and then they launched it toward the goal down at the end of the corridor. They call this the Corridor Principle.

The Corridor Principle is this: you stand at the beginning of the corridor, and at the end there's the target, which is a successful, highly profitable business. You start moving down the corridor toward the goal. Almost inevitably, barriers appear, barriers that you could not see when you started off. It was almost as if doors would slide shut, and you can't continue in the direction you were going, but as each barrier slides shut in front of you, a new door would open to the right or the left.

The entrepreneurs would go down a new hallway, and they could see their goal down the new hallway—a new product or service or possibility. They would start moving down it, and again, the door would shut for all kinds of reasons. The economy would go into recession. They'd run out of money. The product or service would become obsolete. And another door opened up.

Each time the entrepreneurs moved down the corridor of opportunity toward their goal, a door would close, and a new door would open. It was almost like going through a maze, but you could never see the door that was going to close until you got to it. You could never see the new door that was opening until you got to the closed door.

Eventually, after weeks, months, years, they'd finally arrive at their goal at the end of the corridor, and they'd have a successful, thriving, prosperous business. The person would be wealthy and esteemed and respected.

These people said that the most important part of the entire process was to launch in the first place and start moving down the corridor. The major reason people fail is they always have an excuse not to launch. It's not quite the right time, not quite the right place—maybe next month or next year. The great majority of the MBAs, 90 percent, just went to work for wages.

This Corridor Principle is the great principle of success. Just launch, just start, just start moving, and, as long as your are consistent in your application of the 6 Essentials we discussed in this book, every door will open. Every resource will appear, and you cannot see any of them as you're moving out. They'll almost all be unexpected, and yet you just keep moving, plodding along.

My friend from Russia went through the most incredible difficulties and privations, and yet he just kept plodding forward. A very nice man, very easygoing, very innocuous. If you met him on the street, you'd think he was a bus driver or a shop clerk, but he had this one quality—he just kept moving forward—and eventually he achieved his goal of great business success. An extraordinary example, but it seems to be true throughout the world, throughout history.

So if you decide that you want to start and build a successful business, launch. The key to success is to get going and keep going: launch and never give up. Never give up, no matter what happens, and bounce back. Pick yourself up and keep going, just like a football player who gets knocked down. You keep getting up.

As Confucius said, it's not how many times you get knocked down, but how many times you stand up again and keep moving forward, because if you keep standing up and moving forward, your success is absolutely inevitable, absolutely guaranteed.

The opportunities for you to achieve success become greater and greater as you move down the corridor. You learn more and more. You have more and more insights. You develop greater and greater self-confidence. You make more contacts with more people who can help you, and the most extraordinary things happen.

Final Words of Wisdom for Entrepreneurs:

1. There is more opportunity to be successful in business than has ever existed in human history.

2. You can learn anything you need to learn to be successful in business.

3. You can do it—you have more capabilities than you could use in a hundred lifetimes.

4. Make a decision to never give up.

5. Practice the Corridor Principle—and move toward the goal at the end of the corridor.

9 781722 506445